Boyhood Along The Brook Called Horn

William. F. Jeter

HARA
PUBLISHING GROUP

**Published by
Hara Publishing
P.O. Box 19732
Seattle, WA 98109**

Copyright ©2003 by
William. F. Jeter

ISBN: 1-887542-03-5

Library of Congress Catalog Card Number:
2003105498

Manufactured in the United States
10 9 8 7 6 5 4 3 2

Editor: Vicki McCown
Illustrations: William. F. Jeter
Cover Design: Scott Fisher
Cover Photo: L. Everett Jeter
Book Design & Production: Scott and Shirley Fisher

Acknowledgments

First, please realize that I make no claims to being a "writer" per se. If anything, I can be called a "rememberer." I just stumbled onto the fact that nearly nothing is forgotten, and ended up spending many a happy sunrise recalling my small town roots.

These writings exist because of a few folks who encourage me to keep on remembering.

My lifetime friend, Frank Fick, read every chapter. We would then sit for hours and chat about our boyhoods in the mountains. These sessions made me realize that my writing would resurrect many happy memories in the minds of my readers.

A long time Yreka friend, Bill Potter, also read every word and encouraged me to continue. In that Bill is a voracious reader, his opinions were important to me.

My wife, was a dedicated reader who served as a sounding board and provided motivation for me to keep on keeping on. Actually, I could have kept on for another year, but I had to stop somewhere.

If you grew up in the "country," this book will fill your head with memories. If you didn't, it will let you in on what you missed—life as it was meant to be lived, at least in the forties in the mountains of California.

Table of Contents

Prologue

In the very northernmost part of California, where Interstate 5 passes through, lies the Cottonwood Creek Valley. The creek gathers melted snow from Southern Oregon's Siskiyou Mountains and gurgles along in a southerly direction until it flows into the Klamath River.

Because the Spanish didn't get much farther north than San Francisco and the inland settlers, like John Bidwell and Peter Lassen, tended to remain in the fertile Sacramento River Valley, there were very few white men in this part of California before 1830.

Prior to the white man, the Shasta Indians must have found this little valley a pleasant place to live. The mountains on both the east and west sides of the Cottonwood Basin yielded an ample supply of deer, bear, mountain lion, bobcat, and rabbit for food and fur clothing. The creek itself watered a boundless supply of blackberry bushes and provided a windfall glut of migrating salmon every autumn. To top it all off, the foothills to the east and the valley floor contained a yearly harvest of acorns.

Fur trapping probably brought the first white men to the area. In the late 1830s we know that the Hudson Bay Company contracted with one Peter Skene Ogden to open a trapper's trail along the Klamath River in this area.

Some time during 1841, a U.S. Government exploration team passed through the valley on the old Hudson Bay Company trail. This particular group was making an overland exploration trip from Vancouver, B.C. to the San Francisco area.

Several years after the 1848 discover of gold at Sutter's Mill, eager gold miners began to work their way into these far northern mountains. In 1851 gold was discovered in the Valley, and "Cottonwood Diggens" (named for the trees along the creek) soon became a thriving little settlement.

Once the gold was depleted, the townspeople took a look around and discovered that the valley was a good place to do some farming and tree cutting. By this time, the miners, with their Winchester rifles, had spilled enough Indian blood so that the Shasta no longer claimed the valley as their own.

By 1866, the area was home to a genuine little town with stores and saloons and even a post office. The townspeople wanted officially to name their settlement "Cottonwood," but found that the name was already taken by a community "down below." So they named their town "Henley" after a prominent citizen who was evidently their state senator.

In the late 1800s, the railroad began to extend its iron fingers northward from the Sacramento Valley. In 1887, a local rancher, David Horn, sold his land on the east side of Cottonwood Creek as railroad right of way. As could be expected, part of the town shifted across the creek to the railroad tracks and the name "Hornbrook" was given to that new settlement.

For about thirty years, Hornbrook was a booming railroad town. Locomotives and their crews were stationed here to help push freight trains over the mighty Siskiyou mountains to Oregon. Cafés and saloons, and even a hotel, were built to serve the passenger trains that stopped to take on water and coal. Because Oregon was a "dry" state, a great deal of whiskey was sold to southbound passengers, especially during World War I when the big troop trains stopped.

Unfortunately, the railroad saw wisdom in bypassing the Siskiyous with a new eastern route. In 1927, the "Natron Cut-Off" at Weed was opened. Traffic through Hornbrook dwindled considerably and some seventy railroading families were transferred out of town as a result. Again, the area settled back to being a farming and timber community.

In the mid-thirties, a large fire contributed to the shrinkage of the town by consuming much of the downtown area.

Thanks to the big mill in the town of "Hilt" (six miles to the north), there was steady work to be had in the timber industry. During the fifties and early sixties, Hornbrook even had its own sawmill and a planing mill—but the mills didn't last long. By 1973 even the big mill in Hilt had closed down.

Hornbrook's beauty has always been the fact that it was a quiet mountain town, and it continues to live up to that reputation as we enter the 1990s.

Chapter One

The World's Greatest Birthday Party

I whistled a little tune as I pulled on my best school blue jeans. I felt very excited because today was the day that Charley Skimp was having his birthday party, and I truly loved birthday parties.

Next, I took out my Sunday school shirt, buttoned it up very carefully, and tucked it into the jeans. To top it all off, I pulled on leather oxfords, then attached a rabbit's foot key chain to one of my front belt loops.

Now it was Mom's turn to get in on the act. She moistened a wash rag and wiped my face nice and clean. Then she sprinkled some water on my head and used Dad's hairbrush to arrange my hair nice and neat. Finally, she ordered me into the bathroom to scrub my hands one more time.

With spic and span hands, I could now sit down and finish wrapping the gift we had purchased for the party. Just this morning we had gone down to T. Jones and Company and picked out a bag of marbles for Charley. I liked having marbles around, because if you didn't play with them they always made great ammunition for your sling shot. You couldn't find a stone that would sail through the air as straight and true as a marble.

I dried my hands and yelled to Mom that we could leave now. Together, we walked out the front door and climbed into our black '37 Chevy two-door sedan. I felt real proud about how the Chevy looked, because Dad had just spray painted it. He used a spray gun attachment that came with

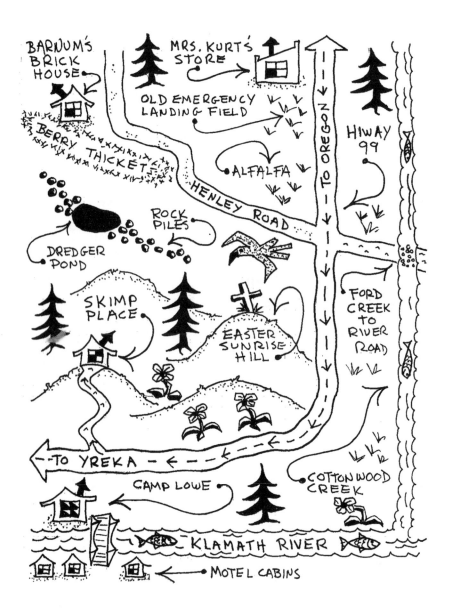

Mom's new canister vacuum cleaner. You just hooked the suction pipe onto the exhaust end of the vacuum and it blew air through the spray gun. Dad said that you couldn't buy new cars during the war, so we had to make this one last.

We had to drive about two miles south on Highway 99 to where Camp Lowe, a fishing resort motel, straddled the Klamath River. It was a warm spring day so Mom and I kept the windows down as we watched the green fields slide by. From time to time, a redwing blackbird would dart across the highway in front of us and I saw several red-tailed hawks patiently gliding over their hunting grounds.

Mom signaled with her arm out the window and we turned right off the highway directly across from Camp Lowe. I hopped out of the Chevy and struggled to open the barbed wire gate in the fence. It was hard work, but I managed to get it open, then closed it after Mom drove through.

She left the Chevy in first gear as we bumped up the rocky road to where the Skimp place sat atop a little hill. From here you could look back south and see the Klamath River. To the east I could see the hill with the Easter Sunrise Service cross standing on top of it. Just a month or so ago we had stood there in the dawn light, listening to our pastor tell us about how Jesus was crucified on the cross and then rose from the dead three days later. Mr. Skimp, who also worked with Dad at the border inspection station, always seemed to live at a place where he could do some farming on the side.

The minute we stopped, Charley and his sister, Elva opened my door and I stepped out onto the running board and handed Charley his gift. Mom stood and chatted with Mrs. Skimp while we happy three ran around to the backyard, where tables and chairs had been set up on the grass.

Every time we heard another car grinding up the rocky hill, we'd run back out front to greet the newcomers. It wasn't long before Tommy Hegler, Elden Francis, Oliver and Frank Fick, and Dickie Fillippe had all arrived. Each time we ran

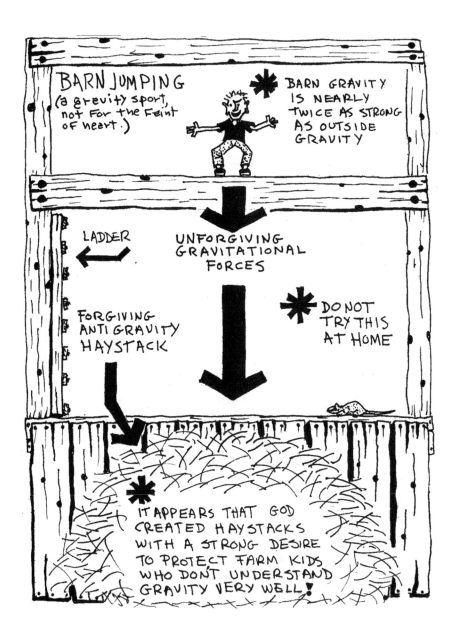

back around the house, we'd find that Mrs. Skimp and Elva had added a few more things to the table.

Finally, we all sat down to big glasses of cherry Kool Aid. Then, we all had some of Mrs. Skimp's homemade ice cream. She had just mixed it up and frozen it in her Frigidaire, so it was crunchy frozen on the top and soft on the bottom.

When the chocolate cake was served, we all ate as if we were pigs. Suddenly Dickie let out a big belch, and we all started giggling and belching and eating like pigs at the same time. It didn't get much better than this.

Charley ripped through the gift opening like an eager buzz saw. That made us all happy, because there was one thought on our collective minds. We all wanted to play; and we all knew that the Skimp place—with its barn and farm animals and rocks and trees—was every kid's dream of the perfect place to play.

We heard the back screen door bang against the wooden frame and looked up to see Mrs. Skimp in her flowered apron. She took a quick look at the table, now littered with gift wrappings, and our faces, with their Kool Aid smiles and chocolate frosting smears. She knew it was time. "Charley," she said, "why don't you take these boys out to play in the barn."

This was it. In a flash we were on our feet and running around the house towards the front gate, with Elva and her red pigtails in the lead. Once we were out the front gate, the barn was just another 20 or 30 yards beyond.

It wasn't a huge barn, but was typical of most, with its bare wood sides and wood shingle roof. On one side there were stalls for the cows and some space for the tractor; the other side was the hay loft and a tool room.

Most barns have a particular smell of their own. As we entered this one, our noses met with a mixture of the sweet smell of oat hay, the musky odor of dry cow manure, and the scent of sun-baked wood. Cracks in the walls and roof admitted bright shafts of sunlight that pierced the shadowy interior. A barn was a great place to be.

I paused for a second or two while my eyes adjusted to the patterns of light and dark. Before the rest of us could really decide what to do next, Charley had already started climbing a ladder that was nailed to one of the main supports for the roof.

We watched closely as he reached the top, spread his arms, and slowly balanced his way out onto one of the big cross beams. If there was ever a born barn climber, it was for sure Charley Skimp. He paused for a moment, took aim at the heaping pile of oat straw below, and then launched himself into space. We all lost sight of him, as the straw gently absorbed his falling body with a soft crunching sound.

Then we all started climbing and jumping into the haystack. Once I even tried to make my way up to the highest beam where Charley had jumped from the first time. I got up the ladder all right, but when I started walking out onto the beam, I got so scared that my stomach felt as if it was trying to climb into my throat. With quivering legs, I retreated downwards to a lower beam and leaped butt first into the waiting haystack.

It was great fun. We leaped and yelled and jumped and screamed until we lay exhausted in the straw.

In the momentary silence, I could hear a couple of horse flies buzzing around overhead. Outside, a cow started noisily lap-lapping water from a trough. Hearing the cow noises from outside seemed to energize Charley. He jumped to his feet and ordered us all outside to the corral so that we could see his new calf. We had all seen calves before, but none of us actually had a private one in our own backyard.

Trailing bits and pieces of straw, the whole gang followed Charley outside. I stood squinting in the bright sunlight for a moment or two. Then, like the others, I climbed onto the top rail of the corral fence to get a good view of the little white-faced calf.

Charley hopped through the fence and scampered around until he was able to get his arms around the animal's neck. Then he asked me if I wanted to take a little ride. Overjoyed to be first, I quickly scrambled through the fence. I made my way around the fresh manure piles to the calf, who looked much bigger now that I stood right next to it.

I threw my right leg up onto the little critter's back and then pulled myself up until I sat squarely in the middle of his back. So far, so good. I figured we'd have a little walk around the corral and then someone else could take a turn. But, Charley had an entirely different idea about what a ride should be. Before I knew what was happening, he ran around to the back of my mount, grabbed its tail, and twisted it a time or two.

All of a sudden, what I thought would be a kind of a pony ride rapidly changed into a full-scale rodeo. The calf was not at all happy with this tail twisting business. He figured that, if he could just buck me off his problem would be solved.

The more he hopped and bucked and jumped, the more Charley laughed and twisted that tail. No matter how hard I held on, I knew it would be only a matter of seconds before he'd succeed in bucking me off. In my bouncing brain, the biggest problem seemed to be all those fresh cow pies, just lying there waiting to welcome me back to the hard ground.

Finally, my hands slipped and I went flying, hitting the ground on my back. As I stood there scraping cow manure off my sleeve, I suddenly became aware of everyone else laughing so hard tears were streaming down their cheeks. I started laughing too, and the rodeo quickly continued. No one wanted to miss out on having a ride. Charley seemed more than happy to provide the tail twisting and the cow pies appeared more than able to cushion our falls. Each time a new victim bit the dust, we gave him a big cheer and laughed until our sides hurt.

We were having such a great time; it seemed for a while that time stood still. Then, all of a sudden, I heard our Chevy grinding its way up the hill. I couldn't believe the day was over and Mom had arrived to drive me home. Slowly, we all plodded back towards the house, trailing bits of straw and cow manure.

When I climbed into the front seat of the car, Mom seemed to notice right away that I didn't look quite as neat as I did when she dropped me off. My face was smeared with chocolate frosting and Kool Aid, pieces of straw suck out of my hair, and my best Sunday school shirt was stained with dirt and manure. She wrinkled her nose, smiled a little, and said, "Well, it looks like you had a good time." I answered her with a tired grin.

As we bumped back down the hill, I let out a big sigh and looked in the side mirror for a last glimpse of the hay-filled barn. Yep, I really did have a great time. This just might have been the world's greatest birthday party.

Chapter Two

The Woodshed Toy Store

Quickly, I rinsed my breakfast dish and stacked it on the drain board with the other dirty dishes. Mom had filled us full of French toast this morning—one of my favorite things to eat. It was Saturday morning and Saturday mornings were extra sweet because it meant freedom from school and memorizing those dreaded times tables.

I felt excited and rushed because something kind of special had happened at our house last week. Every October everyone in Hornbrook had to make sure their woodsheds were filled to the rafters with winter firewood. Just last Tuesday afternoon, a rickety old Ford V-8 dump truck had deposited our stock of winter fuel out behind the woodshed.

Dad and I spent several evenings throwing and shoveling the blocks into the shed, so it wouldn't get rained and snowed on as the weather turned colder.

My excitement arose from the fact that this wasn't just any old kind of firewood. This wood was Hilt wood. Hilt was located five or six miles up the highway, towards Oregon. The whole town was built around a giant saw mill box factory owned by The Fruit Growers.

This was not just firewood. It was a giant stack of building blocks. I had a year-long source of soft pine blocks for whittling and an endless supply of perfectly sized building material, just waiting to be hammered and sawed into whatever toys my imagination could come up with.

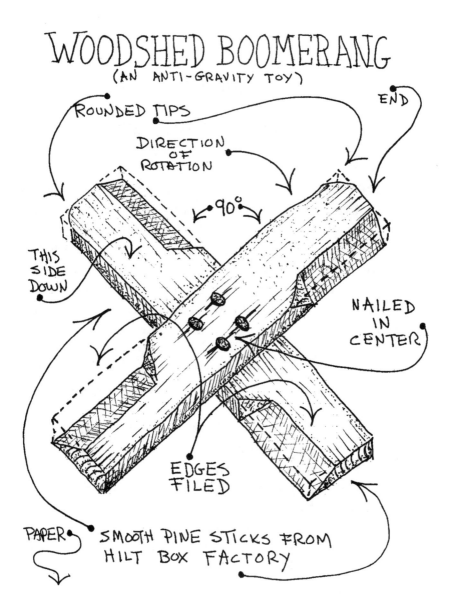

WOODSHED BOOMERANG
(AN ANTI-GRAVITY TOY)

ROUNDED TIPS

END

DIRECTION
OF
ROTATION

90°

THIS
SIDE
DOWN

NAILED
IN
CENTER

EDGES
FILED

PAPER

SMOOTH PINE STICKS FROM
HILT BOX FACTORY

I dried my hands, pulled on a warm flannel shirt, and headed out the back door. It didn't take long for my eight-year-old legs to carry me across the flagstone walkway that led to the waiting woodshed. As I opened the squeaky wooden door and stepped inside, the fresh pine-tar smell of the wood filled my nostrils. I liked the smell of fresh cut wood, so I just stood there and enjoyed it for a moment.

Because there were so many blocks of so many different sizes—all so smooth and square—I was quickly able to pick out a few pieces to work with. Carefully, I made a neat little stack, cradled it in my arms, and carried it next door to our garage, which doubled as my Dad's workshop.

Our workshop was rather cluttered and messy, but I liked to be there. I was happy to have a dad who would let me use his tools any time I wanted to.

My immediate plan was to build a boomerang to play with. To do this, I had selected two pieces of wood about 14 inches long, 2 inches wide, and 1/2 inch thick. First, I needed to nail the two together exactly in the middle in a cross pattern. Then I'd take Dad's wood rasp and smooth the opposite edges down, so that it looked kind of like a four-bladed airplane propeller.

Once my work was complete, I could take it to the field out in front to play with. When held by the end of one blade and given a good sidearm fling, a good woodshed boomerang would cut a smooth curving arc through the air.

As I tightened the vice around one of my hunks of wood, I noticed a strange sound. Except for the odd barking dog and an occasional rooster crowing, Hornbrook always seemed to be a quiet place on a Saturday morning.

I stopped working, cocked my head towards the sound, and listened a bit more intently. It was still faint, but it sounded a bit like a room full of mountain lions, growling deep in their throats. All of a sudden, it hit me; this was the rumble of big military airplane engines.

I dropped my tools, sprang out the garage door, and ran full tilt around the house to the front yard. The rumbling, growling noise became louder and louder as I ran. Now, for sure, I knew it had to be two big radial engines roaring down on us from the north. They had to be really low to be so loud.

I burst through the front gate skidded to a stop on the gravel, and there they were. My skin crawled with excitement, as my eyes locked on to two Grumman Avenger Torpedo bombers, screaming down the railroad tracks at tree top level. In an instant, my wide eyes captured their shiny midnight-blue paint with white stars on the sides, and I could clearly see the pilots and rear gunners as they thundered by.

Once they got to the Southern Pacific Railroad Depot, they roared up into the sky. Then they were gone. All of a sudden, the silence was deafening.

Every boy in my school would have given a million dollars to be old enough to join the Marines and fly off to Okinawa or Iwo Jima and drop bombs on the Japanese ships. Since the Marines weren't taking many third graders, however, we had to be content with our dreams.

We heard stories about Willy Jones's big brother, "Speed," who was a real Marine, and Kenny and Charley Dailey, who were lucky enough to have a dad who was a real sailor serving in the Pacific. Dad always told me that he had been too young for World War I and too old for World War II. I knew for sure that I was too young, but I dreamed all the time about flying a P-51 Mustang or a P-38 Lightning in the war.

Slowly, I turned and shuffled back towards the house. By this time, Mom and my two sisters, Sally and Ann, were out on the front porch trying to catch a glimpse of the rapidly vanishing Grummans. Mom said that the pilots were probably lost and had buzzed the depot so they could see our town name, which was posted on both ends of the roof.

My heart was still thumping with excitement as I walked back to the garage.

As I returned to work on my boomerang, I tried just a bit harder to make it look like a four-bladed airplane propeller. I even rounded the tips a bit as a final touch. I figured that, if I filed the edges just right, it would lift itself high into the sky just like the propellers on those big blue Grummans.

With my creation complete and tightly clutched in my right hand, I headed down the road to the field in front of Willy's house. As my feet crunched along on the gravel, I heard a screen door slam. Looking to my left, I saw that Elden Francis was just coming out to play with his bow and arrow. (He liked to shoot arrows straight up into the sky, and then see how close they would land to the place from where he shot them,) We were both happy to have somebody else to play with.

The fall air was crisp and clear and we two friends began to have a great time together. I'd sail my new toy into the air and Elden would try to shoot it with an arrow. Then, he'd shoot an arrow and I'd try to hit it in flight with my boomerang.

After a while, Mom yelled at us, and we took an afternoon break for some cherry Kool Aid on my front porch. We licked our lips and went right back to shooting and throwing things into the sky. What would we do for fun if we didn't have the sky to play with?

All of a sudden the sun was slipping down behind Cottonwood Peak, and Dad was yelling for me to come home for dinner. Reluctantly, I trudged towards home, with my now dented and battered toy in hand. I hated to quit playing, but the thought of one of Mom's dinners kept me moving along.

As I entered the house, the sweet aroma of hamburger steaks with chopped onions urged me towards the kitchen. Mom had a friendly, warm fire in our little kitchen stove to ward off the autumn chill. She looked up from her big cast

16

iron skillet, smiled, and pointed her spatula towards the wood box behind the stove. Darn! The box was empty and it was my job to fill it on a daily basis.

In the fading light of sunset, I hurried back to the shadowy woodshed. I stacked my arms high with the same pine blocks that just a few hours before had been building blocks for my toys. I didn't worry about burning my favorite building material, because a juicy hamburger steak with onions and boiled potatoes was rapidly becoming the most important thing in my world.

Chapter Three

Jacobs' Hill: Blueprint for Fun

My sleepy-sleepy brain knew that it was morning, but it was a dark and cold winter morning. Because no one in Hornbrook had insulation in their houses and because stove oil "cost too much," Mom and Dad didn't bother to heat our bedrooms.

With three inches of snow on the ground and February on the calendar, my unheated bedroom was a chilly place to be. I knew it was Saturday and that meant "play" instead of "school." But my body kept saying, "Just curl up tight in these warm flannel sheets and everything will be okay in the entire universe."

I heard the clunk of heavy metal from the kitchen and knew that meant that Mom was stuffing wood into the little stove attached to our hot water heater. Having a mom who got up early to start the fire kind of took the edge off having an ice box for a bedroom. Soon, the tantalizing smell of T. Jones & Company bacon, frying in Mom's big black iron skillet, drifted into my dark domain. My stomach began to realize that I needed some body fuel.

With a burst of youthful energy, I threw the covers back, grabbed my blue jeans and flannel shirt off the cold linoleum floor, and ran through the bedroom door to the dining room. This middle room of our house held the oil-fueled heating stove. Quickly, I threw my cold clothing on top of the stove and stood shivering—trying to find some heat for my body as well.

Once dressed and in the kitchen, life began to take on a rosier hue, as the little wood stove made things downright cozy. For some reason, a wood fire always seemed to be friendlier than an oil fire.

Because Mom was cooking bacon, I knew she would want me to run out to the chicken pen for some fresh breakfast eggs. I laced up my high-top leather shoes and ran coatless to the chicken house to see if our little Japanese Banty hens had earned their keep overnight.

Quickly I grabbed three small white eggs and ran shivering back to the warm kitchen. I wasn't really that nuts about fried eggs, but Hornbrook moms were convinced that having a hot meal on a winter morning was a life or death issue; so I had to eat that darn egg.

As I wiped the last bit of egg yolk from my chin, I heard the sound of stomping feet on the wooden floor of our front porch. I opened the front door to find my friends, Oliver and Frank Fick, busily kicking snow off their winter boots. They had drug their sled all the way across town so we could play in the snow together. They were good friends, and I was happy to see them because today was going to be a great day for sledding.

We walked back to the warm kitchen and found that Mom had poured two cups of hot chocolate for my friends. Frank put on his best grin, which revealed a chipped front tooth. (A few months ago, Oliver had thrown a pretend hand grenade at Frank and a tooth got chipped in the process.) We all stood around the little wood stove, talking about what a good day it looked like for sledding and how great the hot chocolate tasted.

Eager to get started, I gulped the last of my warm drink and went into my bedroom for my cold weather stuff. First, there were my wool mittens, scarf, and stocking—all knitted by Mom as a Christmas present. Next, I grabbed my wool, navy blue P-coat, with the deep pockets and warm, turned-up collar. The coat was genuine U.S. Navy war surplus and I was quite proud of it. On the front porch I pulled my buckle galoshes over my leather boots, tucking my jeans into the tops before fastening the last buckle.

I double-checked to make sure that I had a hunk of Mom's paraffin wax in my pocket. Then, I gave my sled a kick to break it loose from the frozen snow. Single file we headed out the front gate and up the street towards Jacobs' Hill. As we walked, the squeak-squeaking noise our boots made in the snow told us the ground was frozen and icy, a great day for sledding.

There were lots of hills around Hornbrook, but Jacobs' Hill always seemed to be very special for us. It was close to our houses—all you had to do was climb a fence to get to it. Mr. Jacobs never seemed to feel that he needed to put "No Trespassing" signs all over it. As hills went, it was just the right size—not too small for the big kids and not too big for the little kids.

This particular hill also had a bit of everything that we liked: wild flowers in the spring; bushes to play cowboys and Indians in; rocks to stand on with your kite string in hand; a smooth side for sledding; and an irrigation ditch that flowed around the front to separate us from the rest of the world. The greatest thing was that we all felt the hill belonged to us, which never seemed to bother Mr. Jacobs very much.

We helped each other pass our sleds over the fence and began to crunch our way up the hill. Halfway up, the sun began to pry its way between the heavy gray clouds that hung low and cold in our valley. Like a magic wand, the sudden shafts of sunlight transformed the snow-covered trees and bushes into a brilliant white storybook land. There seemed to be millions of tiny prisms frozen to everything; the sunlight danced and glittered, with a life of its own.

We had seen the beauty of a snowscape before, but this sudden change stunned us for a moment. We just stood there and stared at the neighborhood below while our lungs

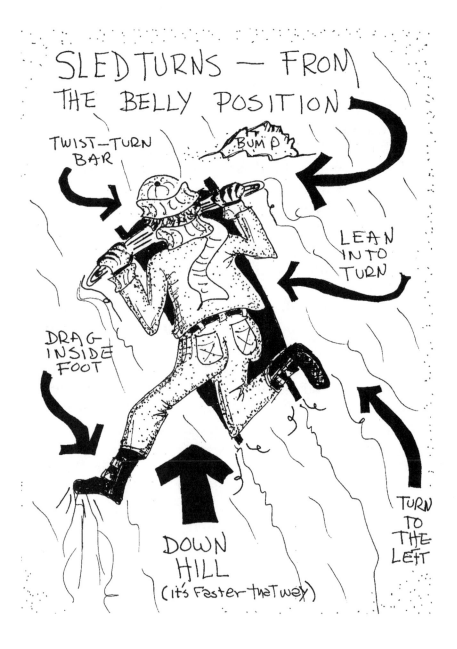

transformed the crispy air into little puffs of fog. Without really knowing what was happening, we allowed our memories slowly to absorb this display of God's brilliance. We then turned to complete our climb to the top of the hill.

The sledding part of Jacobs' Hill was the back side. Here there were no bushes or rocks and no ditch at the bottom. There were steeper and faster hills nearby, but this was our favorite slope because it didn't have any hazards and it only took ten minutes to get there. Before doing anything else, we dug into our pockets for the paraffin blocks we had "borrowed" from our moms' canning supplies. We then waxed the sleds' metal runners for top speed.

We had two basic positions or techniques we used on a flexible-flyer sled. The first technique was mostly for little kids—or girls—and consisted of sitting upright on the sled and operating the steering bar with your feet. This method could be exciting on a real steep hill with my little sister, Ann, clutching on behind me; but you could easily lose control and flip over if you hit a bump. We'd never come right out and admit it, but crashing in the snow was part of the fun of this sport, so we didn't complain about that very much.

The "real man's way" of doing this thing was "belly whomping." You positioned your sled, then leaned forward, placing your hands on both sides. You took four or five running steps to get up some speed, then you flopped belly down on the moving sled and quickly moved your hands to the steering bar.

Life quickly got very exciting from this position, with your nose a mere ten inches from the snow. It seemed as if you were going a hundred miles per hour, as the frosty air ripped at your face. In the belly position, you had less wind resistance and a lower center of gravity, so it was much easier to survive the bumps, which sometimes caused your sled to go completely airborne.

Turns for a good sledder were a combination of using the turning bar like a bicycle handle bar and dragging your foot in the inside of the turn. You also had to apply some body English toward the inside of the turn.

When you really got going on a steep slope, the icy wind tore at your nostrils. You had to hold on like hell to stay on the sled, as the bumps pounded the breath right out of your lungs. When you got to the bottom of the hill, your eyes and nose were running all over your frostbitten face. Your lungs were gasping for breath, and you usually had icy cold snow up your pant legs. We knew one thing for sure, though; this was life the way it was meant to be lived.

No one kept track of time on Jacobs' Hill, so lunch wasn't a matter of schedule. Lunch was a matter of being so tired, wet, frozen, and hungry that you just could not pull that sled back up the hill one more time. With wet mittens and stocking caps stuffed into our jacket pockets, we headed our cold feet toward my house. We hoped that the little wood stove in the kitchen would still be burning brightly.

We leaned our sleds against the side of the house and sat on the front porch so we could pry off our rubber galoshes. This last little job was the key to getting inside, and the darn buckles always seemed to fight back when your hands were cold and stiff. Finally, we got the bulky overshoes off, brushed the snow from our clothes, and stepped into the warm house.

We walked back to the kitchen to find that Mom had brewed up a pot of her quick and easy chili beans, knowing that a hot lunch was just what we'd need. As I spooned the warm spicy food into my hungry mouth, I was one contented kid. Today I had two good friends, a great place to sled, and a mom who loved me with chili beans for lunch.

Crunchy white snow made January and February a magical time, but the later days of winter were a different story. Melting snow and cold, cold rains meant that every place I liked to go was covered with mud. It was a season for staying inside, reading books, and building models.

This was the time of year that my dad would (I hoped) bring home a bundle of long thin sticks that had been cut out of white pine on somebody's table saw. These were more than nice-smelling pieces of wood; these were the basic raw materials for our spring kites. With some help from Dad, my sisters and I could now begin to create our spring kites. While the winter rains pounded on our sometimes leaky roof, I'd cut the sticks to length and tie them carefully together with string from the family string ball.

My favorite kite was the box kite. Box kites were big, square, and strong looking. To create something like this with my own two hands—and have it actually rise into the sky—was a wonderful and mysterious thing.

Once I had the sticks (thanks to Dad), all I needed was some brightly colored tissue paper from T. Jones & Company, a bottle of mucilage, scissors, and the family string ball.

First, I had to slog through the mud to the garage where we had our work bench and tools. There, I'd put the sticks in Dad's vise and cut little string notches in the ends of the four main sticks. Next, I'd carefully cut V-shaped grooves in the ends of my four diagonal cross braces.

With the sticks shaped, it was now a matter of carefully tying and gluing the structure together. After the glue dried, I'd take Mom's sewing scissors and carefully cut some red tissue paper to size. I then folded the paper around the strings that went from corner to corner of the frame and glued it with mucilage.

Without realizing it, I had just reinvented heavier-than-air flight, in much the same way Chinese boys did hundreds of years before the Wright Brothers spent their rainy evenings building a man-carrying kite with a motor on it.

Now there was "waiting" to be done. It seems I was always waiting for something. I waited for Christmas to come so I could get some toys. I waited for it to snow so I could

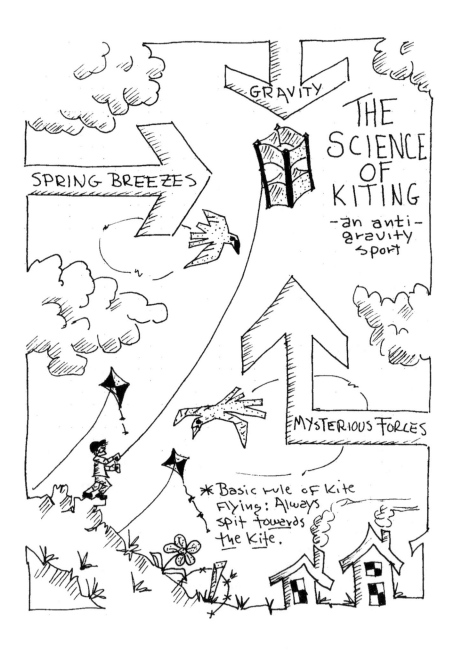

sled. I waited for it to get warm enough so I could swim in the creek. And now I had to wait out the last shreds of winter before I could launch my beautiful new kite. In the meantime, it sat patiently in the corner of my bedroom.

I'm not sure exactly how we knew when springtime finally arrived. Usually Mom would be washing the breakfast dishes; she would look out at the back lawn and exclaim something like, "Look, there's the first robin of springtime."

The first robin was quickly followed by the sprouting of the pussywillows along Cottonwood Creek. Then the rain storms would begin to feel more like they were threatening to turn things green instead of threatening to cover things with snow. Deep in my heart I'd know that God was beginning to create new life all over the countryside—and we always felt excited about that.

One Saturday morning I just knew this had to be the first day of kite season. It was still cool but the winter chill had left, the ground looked damp, but not muddy, and (most important of all) a steady north wind began to blow. The deep blue sky was landscaped with an ever changing flock of puffy white clouds and it just seemed to be crying out to be filled with kites.

Because kite flying was always best in the afternoons, I spent the morning doing a few chores and giving my creation a last-minute check-up. My little sister had a "store-bought" kite, which I helped to "get together" and rig up the right way.

Because the wind was fairly strong, something else was needed. I went to the family rag bag on the back porch and found some colorful cotton scraps, which I tore into strips and knotted together for a tail. (Tails added something to the look of the kite. They also helped store-bought kites fly steady and upright when the wind got too strong.)

Once the tail was done, I made another trip to the back porch to find the string winders that Dad made for us the previous year. He cut out a piece of pine board about four inches by six inches square and nailed an eight-inch piece of broom stick on either end facing opposite directions.

You grasped a broomstick handle in each hand and cranked the string in or out. It worked a lot better than the little cardboard rolls the string came on, and because the string winder was a two-handed affair, the wind never jerked the string out of your hands.

Right after lunch, I grabbed my kite and headed for Jacobs' Hill. All the way out through the woodshed and up the back street, I was testing the wind and watching the clouds as they drifted by. You had to be careful climbing through the barbed wire fence that circled Jacobs' Hill; a sudden gust of wind could blow your kite into the wire and rip the heck out of it.

As I eagerly climbed the hill, the smells of early spring rushed past my nose. The brisk coolness of the wind reminded me that there was still snow high in the Siskiyou Mountains. Carefully, I held my kite upright and downwind, making it weathervane with the wind as I walked.

You had to recognize that the kite was already partially in its natural environment and I let it do what the wind told it to do. Otherwise, a gust could blow it out of your hand and break a stick or rip the paper. Breaking a home-built kite before you even had a chance to let it fly was a sad experience—one that I wanted to avoid this spring day.

By the time I arrived, several other kids already stood on top of the hill, including my big sister, Sally, and my little sister, Ann. I didn't pay much attention to them because kite flying always seemed a solitary sort of activity for me. Once on top of the hill, I chose a rock to stand on— one that wasn't too close to the others because I didn't want to tangle my string with someone else's.

I felt rather nervous because this first flight of the season would put my building skills to the test. Carefully, I let out about six feet of string, felt the wind steady on the back of my head, then gently committed my creation to the unseen wind currents. The tissue paper rattled in protest, as a sudden gust grabbed at its sides and began to pull the thing skyward. Quickly I let out some more string. She paused for a moment, then eagerly bolted skyward with new found freedom. The more string I gave to her, the more she soared towards the clouds. Now I knew for sure that I had built one great kite.

As I slowly cranked out ever more string, my bright red-and-yellow creation continued its journey ever higher into the heavens. The strange part about all of this was that a part of me—a part of my mind—seemed to be soaring into the puffy white clouds along with my kite. The string acted as an extension cord, plugging me into the sky.

I stood there for an hour or so with my body on top of Jacobs' Hill and my spirit high in the sky, gently supported by the cool spring breezes. Eventually, darkness and dinner time came and I had to go back down the hill to the real world of homework to be done and firewood to be chopped. I knew, though, that I would sleep a happy sleep tonight. Today on Jacobs' Hill I had reached out and touched the clouds.

In a few short weeks, the air grew warmer. The steady rays of the sun produced a profusion of green leaves and wild flowers on the hills that stood around our town. Mom was justly proud of her daffodils and tulips, which had burst out of the warming earth to decorate our yard with welcome splashes of color.

The flowers in our yard were pleasing, and the flowers in the store windows in nearby Yreka were impressive, but everyone in my town knew that there was something extra special about wildflowers. Wildflowers were public domain; you didn't have to plant them, you didn't have to water them, and they had a way of surprising you where you least expected them to be.

THE WILDFLOWER CYCLE
(revealed for the first time on these pages)

GOD places Flowers in secret places.

Little Kids Find Flowers using little Kid instinct.

Little Kids carry armloads of Flowers to their moms.

Moms bake chocolate cakes, using mom instinct, energizing little kids to go Flower hunting.

Wildflowers must be one of God's special gifts to little kids. They only grow in little-kid territory and little kids, like my sister Ann, instinctively knew where to find them. She and the other little kids hiked up to the friendly flanks of Jacob's Hill where they carefully picked handfuls of blue lupines and purple snake heads. They then proudly carried their collections of color down the hill as special gifts for their moms. Hornbrook moms instinctively knew that wildflowers from the hands of little kids brought something special. Their hearts told them to get out their special vases and make sure that every flower was used to decorate the house.

A mom who had just received a fistload of wildflowers from Jacobs' Hill was one happy mom and could always be trusted to bake a chocolate cake within twenty-four hours.

As the lush days of spring faded into the golden brown days of summer, our interest in the hill faded. The cool banks of Cottonwood Creek were a better place to be in the summertime. By next fall, though, when the cold rains began to feel like snow, I'd again start thinking about the good times to be found on Jacobs' Hill.

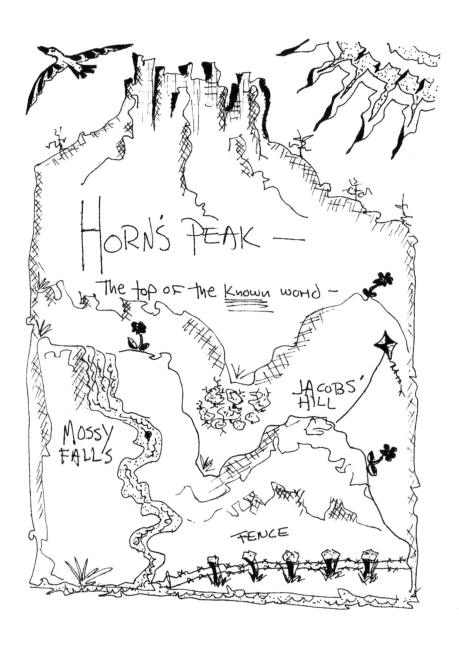

Chapter Four:

Horn's Peak: The Top of the Known World

Swish-ca-chung, swish-ca-chung. It must be Monday morning because this noise from the back porch was the sound of Mom's old washing machine thrashing the dirt out of my blue jeans.

Washing machine noise was nearly as pleasant as the constant chirping of the red-breasted robins in the big locust tree in the front yard. That sound meant Mom was out back, working away to keep her family in clean clothes and that meant that she loved us—it was good to be loved.

The sun's rays seemed to be saying it's mid-morning, but my bed still felt like a good place to be—life was good when you could sleep in all summer long. Thank God no one expected a ten-year-old kid to get up and go to work during summer vacation. That would come soon enough.

My mind wishfully sorted through possible activities for the day. It occurred to me Willy Jones had said something about hiking up to Horn's Peak today. I quickly realized that idea had real possibilities for a day of fun.

Willy lived close by, which was important in Hornbrook because no one had telephones. He was also an enthusiastic hiker, ran a lot, and played baseball. We all knew that Willy would someday play baseball for the New York Yankees. After all, he had the only first base mitt in town and he knew all about Lou Gherig.

If I didn't get up pretty soon, Mom might yell at me to wake up; sleeping in was one thing, but being lazy was another issue all together. I rolled out of my warm nest, pulled on yesterday's knee-patched jeans, grabbed a clean white T-shirt in one hand and my new high-top tennis shoes in the other.

Every kid in Hornbrook was elated to get out of his leather winter shoes and into his brand new summer tennis shoes. Your parents tried to add extra life to your old leather shoes by gluing cat's paw soles over the growing holes, but time and the laws of nature were on our side. These black canvas babies from T. Jones & Company were so light, it seemed that I could run like the wind. Life could be sweet in a new pair of tennis shoes.

The kitchen was empty because my sisters were still sleeping. Mom was out in the backyard doing the thing that made my T-shirts smell so good—hanging them to dry in the fresh morning breeze. With a little bit of luck I could find some fresh strawberries from our garden and a bottle of milk that still had some cream on the top. Cream and strawberries could turn a couple of Shredded Wheat biscuits into a meal fit for a king. A quick glance into the old four-legged Frigidaire confirmed my plans for a breakfast feast.

I crumbled the Shredded Wheat into a bowl, spooned some strawberries on top, poured in some cream, and topped it all off with three heaping spoonfuls of high-energy sugar from far off Hawaii.

As I ate and listened to Mom's little radio play some of the day's top ten songs, I realized that a bit of haste might be in order. Because Monday was the day after Sunday, and because you didn't have to work on Sunday, Mom might think that it was a good day for lawn mowing, weed pulling, or something even worse (like cleaning out the chicken house). It would definitely be smart to get moving before Mom thought of some chore for me to do. If I were gone, maybe she would put my big sister, Sally, to work instead. I smiled at the thought.

34

Out the front door, the screen door slammed BAM! behind me. I rolled out my trusty hand-me-down bike from the side of the house. My bike had been "summerized" by removing the fenders, and it had the only narrow racing bike tires in the whole town. A bike was more important to a Hornbrook kid than anything else in the whole wide world. They could take my toothbrush or my new canvas shoes, but my bike was the very foundation of my life!

After making sure to close the front gate so that wandering cows couldn't invade our yard and feast on Mom's garden, I hopped on the genuine leather seat of my genuine English racing bike for the short down-hill roll to Willy's house. Bike riding had a way of blowing the fuzz out of your eyes in the morning. It felt good to have some wind in my face.

I wheeled up to Willy's house, stood hard on the back pedal, and skidded the rear tire sideways in the gravel. That was a real man's way of stopping, and the experience never seemed to get old. There was Willy, sweating along behind his old push lawn mower in the front yard.

We leaned on opposite sides of the fence laying plans for the day, deciding on a hike up to Horn's Peak. Willy would finish the lawn and then he'd go get his cousin, Tommy, and Billy Paulsen from down the street by the sawmill. We didn't seem to plan things by the clock because no one owned a watch until high school graduation. With a good bike and time to spare, you didn't need a watch anyway.

With the secure knowledge that my day was planned, I realized that the mail truck had probably come and gone by now. I pointed my bike towards the post office to see if Frank and Oliver's grumpy step-dad had the mail sorted into our box yet. No one really wrote to me, but I generated some mail by sending away Wheaties box tops for Japanese toys that never quite worked. Sometimes, I responded to offers for "free information packets" in the

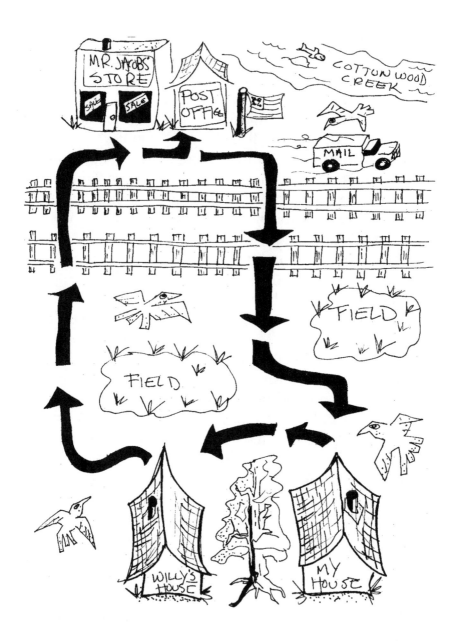

monthly *Popular Mechanics* magazine. Even if I didn't get any mail, going to the post office was still a great thing to do. Everyone knew what time the mail was sorted and made it a daily event to be there.

Because Hornbrook was much too small for a newspaper and nobody had telephones, meeting at the post office was a way of exchanging local gossip. I felt somewhat grown up being part of that. Besides, I might get lucky and see a friend or two who lived beyond normal biking distance while I hung around waiting for Willy to finish his lawn.

It only took a few minutes of bumping my bike over the railroad tracks and dodging potholes in the road. I parked my bike on one of the few sidewalks in town, walked inside the cool post office, and took a peek through the little glass window in P.O. Box 176. A few envelopes were there, but I could hear the rhythmic thunk, thunk, ka-thunk, thunk that meant Mr. Chapman was still sliding mail into our boxes. Realizing that I didn't possess the five cents necessary to buy a comic book from Mr. Chapman's magazine stand, I wandered next door to Mr. Jacobs' store to buy a couple of one-cent Tootsie Rolls.

Now I could perch on the wooden bench out in front of the post office, enjoy my candy, and survey the downtown scene with some degree of luxury. The morning sun felt good, the cool air from Cottonwood Creek behind the post office smelled of blackberries, and the Tootsie Rolls tasted great. I was a contented boy in a clean white T-shirt.

Even though there was no mail for me, I felt good pedaling home with the monthly electricity bill from the California Oregon Power Company and a letter from my Aunt Bessie, who lived "down below" in Southern California. Picking up the mail made me feel as if I had done something for my family. I bounced back across the railroad tracks and up the small hill to our wooden house.

The front door now stood open, as Mom always wanted to capture cool outside air in the house so the afternoon heat wouldn't be too uncomfortable. I headed for the kitchen, realizing that I would need a good bag lunch to eat on top of Horn's Peak.

First, I checked under the sink and retrieved a brown paper bag, which had found its first use bringing groceries home from the T. Jones & Company store. I then went to the fridge for some of Mom's homemade dill pickles. I then got some bread from the tin bread box on the drain board, and grabbed a jar of peanut butter and the wax paper from the cupboard. You just couldn't beat a good peanut butter and dill pickle sandwich on a hike. It also helped to have along a few celery sticks and a couple of Mom's chocolate chip cookies—if I was lucky enough to find them.

I carefully folded the top of the paper bag and set the lunch on the oil cloth covered kitchen table. I needed to locate the rest of my hiking gear on the back porch. The rest of the gear consisted of war surplus stuff like a genuine Marine Corps bayonet and a dented aluminum canteen. The canteen's original owner had scratched a name and place on its sides ("Private Marvin Marshall, Iwo Jima") I wondered briefly if Private Marshall had died there. Both of these items attached to a green surplus cartridge belt, which had been specially adjusted by Dad so that it would fit my skinny hips. I filled the canteen with cool water, grabbed a blue baseball cap, checked my jeans for a Boy Scout knife, and knew I was ready to tackle Horn's Peak.

We met one another in the field in front of Willy's house. After a quick comparison of equipment, we headed up the graveled street towards the hills. As we started, I heard someone shouting, "Wait for me! Wait for me!" It was Norm Burdt from down the river. His dad had dropped him off for a day in town when he came for the mail. Norm was now running across the railroad tracks in his big black engineer's boots, waving and shouting to be included in whatever it was we were going to do.

Norm was always good to have along because he was a fearless hiker and there wasn't anything he wouldn't try at least once. Luckily he had stuffed his jeans pockets with peanuts, candy bars, and Tootsie Rolls, so he was ready to go. I always liked having him around because he was the only kid in our school who was skinnier than I was.

We walked and talked up the street behind my house to Mr. Jacobs' old barn. There we crawled through the barbed wire fence that officially marked the line between "the Town" and "the hills." Once we crossed through this fence, we were in a new world. This world had a whole new set of rules—good rules because they were kids' rules and not parents' rules.

Here you were free to throw rocks at anything that moved, pick flowers, yell, scream, jump in a bush, get your shoes wet, and get your clothes dirty. A kid was free really to be a kid once he crossed through the fence next to Mr. Jacobs' barn. Best of all, there was no admission charge to "the hills."

Just beyond the fence was the irrigation ditch that ran around the base of Jacobs' Hill. We leaped across the water and proceeded along the trail next to the ditch. Without thinking much about it, we each grabbed some rocks and started throwing at random targets in the water as we walked and talked.

I liked to aim at the spider-like insects we called "water skippers" because of the way they darted about on the surface of the water. Mostly, we just chucked rocks into the ditch because we enjoyed the splashing and the casual test of our marksmanship. We only sometimes waded up the ditch; even though this was allowed in your summer tennis shoes, no one wanted to climb Horn's Peak in soggy shoes.

Once we passed the fence that marked the back side of Jacobs' Hill, we walked a bit faster. At this point, the hiking

COWPIE SELECTION CHART

I. THE SIZE TEST—

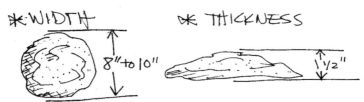

* WIDTH   * THICKNESS

8" to 10"   1 1/2"

II. THE TOUCH TEST—

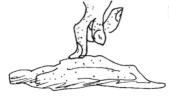

* A proper pie will feel much the same as a day-old cinnamon roll.
* If your finger pierces the surface it's too fresh.

III. THE VISUAL TEST

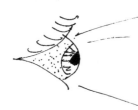

* spinach green – too fresh.
* gray brown – too old.
* dark brown / slight greenish hue – O.K.

REMEMBER – success in a cow pie battle depends on quick and correct ammunition selection.

became fairly easy, the ground rolled along nicely with no steep hills. This kind of land seemed to be favored by the cows that grazed the area, and their many "calling cards" presented us with some immediate fun.

First, Norm picked up a fairly dry cow pie and hurled it discus-style at the group. Norm's throw quickly escalated into a running battle. The basic skill needed in a cow pie battle was the proper selection of ammunition. I sprinted ahead of the group, searching for a proper projectile. A new one would be too messy and the real old ones just crumbled when you tried to throw them. They also had to be fairly flat and round so they would sail through the air when thrown. I quickly found a good pie and sailed it in the general direction of Billy and Tommy.

After a few direct hits, we divided into teams, with Willy and Billy siding against Norm and me. Tommy ended up as sort of a free agent. The air was thick with cow pies and wild shouts of glee. Then Tommy took a heavy hit on the back of the head. Tommy's pain quickly escalated our battle to its worse and messiest level. We now searched for soft ammunition, as we ran across the open area. Because no one really wanted to get hit in the face with a soft cow pie, the battle just fell apart as the clearing blended into a sagebrush-lined trail.

Because we were out of breath, and the narrow cattle trail herded us into a single file, all was quiet as we proceeded through the brush thicket. In addition to providing the ammunition for our cow pie battles, these four-legged friends also provided us with some pretty good trails through the sage brush.

I was content simply to walk along and listen to the distant call of a mountain quail rooster and the nearby screech of ground squirrels as they warned the world of our coming. Like a hunting party of young Shasta Braves, we were happy to see the sights, smell the smells, and hear the sounds. A restful stop at Mossy Falls was our next reward.

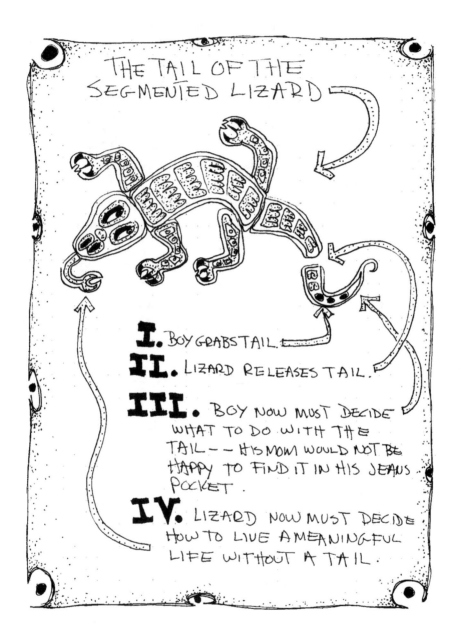

THE TAIL OF THE SEGMENTED LIZARD

I. BOY GRABS TAIL.

II. LIZARD RELEASES TAIL.

III. BOY NOW MUST DECIDE WHAT TO DO WITH THE TAIL -- HIS MOM WOULD NOT BE HAPPY TO FIND IT IN HIS JEANS POCKET.

IV. LIZARD NOW MUST DECIDE HOW TO LIVE A MEANINGFUL LIFE WITHOUT A TAIL.

Up ahead we spotted a rocky outcropping that ran around the hill and through the gully on our left. These rocks and the small creek in the gully combined to create a small waterfall surrounded by sandy ground and small cliffs. We had no idea who had named this spot "Mossy Falls." Probably some gold miner once rested here on a hot summer day, later describing it to a friend as "a mossy falls." That's how places got their names around Hornbrook.

We all ran down the last small hill to the falls. At the creek we lay on our stomachs so we could dip our hot faces in the creek and sip the cool water. As we rested in the shade of a twisted old juniper tree, we couldn't help noticing three or four gray lizards leisurely sunbathing on nearby rocks. (The legend went that they could disconnect their tails to escape, but you had to be fast enough and brave enough to grab the tail to prove this theory.)

We rested and watched until one big daddy lizard scurried right past where we were sitting. In a flash of energy, Billy and Willy took off on hands and knees in a wild attempt to grab the scaly tail. Norm and I ran ahead, stomping our feet in the sandy ground in an attempt to block off the lizard's escape route. After about twenty seconds of frantic chase, daddy lizard dove underneath a large rock to safety. We always said that we wanted a lizard's tail, but the truth was we were afraid to try too hard. Even a fool could see that lizards had teeth.

If we couldn't catch a lizard, we could sure throw rocks at them. We all grabbed fist-sized stones and started throwing them at every reptile in sight. Norm started rolling the big rocks over to expose their hiding places. This worked pretty well, as it forced our targets to scamper to new hiding places. My throwing arm got tired, so I wandered back to the shady creek side. I was soon joined by my four dusty friends. The lizards had won—but that really didn't matter.

Slowly we all got to our feet, realizing that it was now time to start the steep hills. Willy led the way through the scrub oak trees and sagebrush. We walked a few hundred yards when Willy suddenly crouched and began to run. He had spotted several mountain quail running through the underbrush. We spread out and began running forward with Willy.

Suddenly the bushes exploded with roaring wings, as a covey of quail took off like so many gray rockets. They started fast, then set their wings and glided across the gully to a new brush patch. We knew they'd start running the instant they landed, so we didn't bother to follow them—besides, we still had a mountain to climb.

After waiting a few moments for Tommy to catch up with us, we set out again. Going uphill there were no cattle trails to follow because the cows were smart enough to know it was easier to go around the hills. Instead of going straight up, I walked a zig-zag pattern across the face of the hill. I'd look ahead and pick a stone or a patch of grass as a goal, telling myself, "You can rest or have some water when you get to that spot."

Sometimes it helped to put my hands on my knees and push down in an attempt to make my legs work better. Other times I'd grab a stick and use it to push myself up the hill. During that time, none of us talked. We just silently grunted our individual ways up the hill towards the rocky ridge that ran around the top. We were panting and puffing and sweating and loving every minute of it. Because of the rocks, the last few yards were the hardest to climb.

On top we sprawled on our backs on those rocks, gasping and gulping for breath. Overhead I could see several large hawks, drifting in lazy circles on the rising air currents. Hawk watching and resting always seemed to go hand-in-hand. I was fascinated by the effortless way these huge birds seemed to hang in the sky without flapping a wing or twitching a feather. Having hawks or buzzards overhead was kind of like having a kite without string. It was a great excuse to stare at the sky and rest.

44

The clank of Tommy's canteen lid broke the silence. I slowly followed his example, taking a long drink of cool water. As we drank and revived ourselves, our gaze shifted to the view of the valley that now lay at our feet. We were beginning to gain some real altitude and that was an enjoyable thing, due to the ever improving view of the town below.

Norm got up and started wandering up and down the rocky ridge. He knew that our high location meant more than a pleasant view; it meant that we could do some "rock rolling."

Norm found a rock about the size of his head, and checked it on all sides to make sure it was reasonably round. We watched as he grunted the rock to shoulder height and then launched it down the hill with a few quick steps and a big push with both arms. It was a good toss, as the rock hit open ground and started rolling immediately.

I watched with pleasure as God's own gravity worked its magic on the rock. Faster and faster it went, kicking up dust as it bounced and bumped over the cattle trails that crisscrossed the face of the hill. With one final majestic leap, Norm's rock vaulted into a brush patch and suddenly stopped. Several quail burst out of the shaking bushes and glided their way down the canyon. Then, all was quiet.

We quickly forgot our fatigue and decided that this was the perfect place to roll a truly huge boulder. Billy and I grabbed large sticks to use as pry levers as we started searching for the perfect rock—one that was waiting to tumble down the hill with a little encouragement from five eager boys. We settled on a fairly round boulder about two feet high.

Norm and Tommy started pulling smaller rocks away from the downhill side, while Billy and I worked our prying sticks into the dirt on the uphill side. In a few minutes we were ready to give it a try, so we all gathered on the uphill side. Norm pushed with his hands while the rest of us

45

leaned on the prying sticks. Slowly it began to lift from its resting place in the dirt. Norm dropped several fist-sized stones behind it; this held it in place while we got a better bite with our sticks. Again, we leaned on our prying stocks, knowing that this time we would be able to start a majestic rock slide.

Suddenly, a sharp dry rattle-buzzing sound ripped through the air. Our blood froze as fear pulsed through our bodies. Words cannot describe the dry, boney rattling hum that an angry rattlesnake makes. But, once you've heard it, you never ever, ever forget it. Realizing in a flash that we were uncovering a timber rattler's burrow, we quickly let the stone settle back into its resting place.

As much as we loved rock rolling, this took the fun out of it. The only thing I hated more than memorizing the times tables was rattlesnakes, and this one had just been a mere three feet from my skinny ankle. For a moment or two, we just stood there in stunned silence. Then, we started laughing at each other. Billy and I threw our prying sticks in the general direction of the boulder, and moved out towards Horn's Peak, which was looming ever closer behind us. I was determined not to be stopped by a mere brush with death.

Walking rather rapidly now, we traversed a fairly level area of red clay and dry grass. Then, we began the final climb up the rocky slopes of Horn's Peak. Here we could see a wide assortment of stones that had a strange blue color. I pocketed a few, thinking that they just might be the same kind of stones that the Navajo Indians used in making jewelry.

Even though this area was littered with rocks of all shapes and sizes, rock rolling never entered my mind, as I was now obsessed with reaching my goal. The peak itself consisted of some fairly steep rock cliffs. It was difficult going, but our rubber soled shoes, nimble bodies, and eager spirits carried us up and over the cliffs in a few minutes.

Once on top, we just stood there. It was somewhat like walking into a giant cathedral. The view from the top of Horn's Peak demanded silence.

With a cool high country breeze in my sweaty face, I let my eyes drink in the panorama of the valley below. What seemed to be a miniature train chug-chugged through town with a load of logs destined for the big sawmill at Hilt. An equally tiny looking Trailways bus was just entering town from the opposite direction.

As my eyes feasted on this visual meal that my legs had earned, I truly knew that there was no other place in the whole world that I would rather be. Yes sir, Horn's Peak had it all.

Chapter Five

Cottonwood Creek:
A Downtown Wilderness Area

Slowly, I lined up the sights of my nearly new Red Ryder BB gun on a fat, red-breasted robin. Unaware that he was about to "meet his maker," he continued the crime for which he was about to be executed—eating ripe strawberries from my mom's strawberry patch. Gently, I squeezed the trigger until the gun coughed the BB on its well-aimed way. Suddenly, the robin clawed for the sky, leaving a small cloud of feathers behind. Close but not close enough. He'd probably look elsewhere for lunch tomorrow.

Because the berries were ripe and Mom was about ready to can our annual supply of strawberry jam, we were waging war with these feathered fruit robbers. Today I was a "hired gun." I was a bounty hunter with promised earnings of five cents for every robber I could bring to justice. It never worked out to be a high-paying job, but it was great to be paid for playing with my BB gun.

This Red Ryder lever action BB gun was my most prized possession. It wasn't something that had come to me easily, because it cost a lot more than Santa Claus seemed willing to spend on our Christmas presents.

Last summer I worked like a dog, mowing lawns for anyone who would hire me. Through the winter I had a job cutting and stacking firewood for two elderly Indian ladies who lived up the street. Several times my mom and some of the other neighbor ladies had paid me to go out and pick wild blackberries.

It was a lot of hard work, but I saved and saved and saved until that rainy day last April when I walked into T. Jones & Company. I told Mr. Smith that I wanted to buy that Red Ryder he had in his glassed-in toy case (over in the dry goods side of the store). I had looked at it through the glass at least a hundred times, but now it was to be mine—and I earned every darned penny of it.

The sudden screeching of a nearby locust interrupted my daydream. (Locusts singing this early in the morning usually meant that it was going to be a hot day.) The shifting sun was gradually stealing my shade and this little bird-shooting job Mom had thought up for me wasn't turning out to be nearly as exciting as I thought it was going to be. The possibility of doing some exploring along the cool banks of Cottonwood Creek began to sound real good to me. All I had to do was talk my way out of this hired-hunter job.

The screen door on the back of our old wood house went "bang." I looked up to see Mom bringing some kitchen scraps out to the chicken pen. She smiled a little half-smile and asked, "How is it going?" I faked a yawn and told her, "Things are pretty slow, so I guess I've chased those berry robbers away for good this time." Assuming that she'd see it as a clear cut case of a "job well done," I quickly announced, "I was thinkin' about headin' down the creek for a while." When Mom said "Okay," I was suddenly free.

Quickly, I headed around the house and down the road toward the railroad tracks. I whistled a little tune, as I crossed the tracks and headed for the narrow dirt road that cut through the blackberry bushes across from the big yellow house that belonged to the railroad foreman.

We all knew that kids in big cities like Yreka and Ashland had parks and public swimming pools to play in. But that didn't bother us a whole lot; right smack in the middle of town we had good old Cottonwood Creek.

Sometimes in the winter, parts of it would freeze, leaving ice thick enough to slip and slide on. Sometimes the spring rains and the snow thaw caused the old creek to triple its size. When it flooded, it was really exciting just to stand on one of the bridges and watch the awesome power of the surging muddy water.

More than once during high water, I had put my name and address into a bottle and tossed it into the roaring waters. I was sure that the bottle would make its way to the Klamath River, past Happy Camp, and on to the Pacific Ocean. (I hoped that someone's daughter would find it on the beach and send me a postcard.)

As I wandered down the little sandy lane that led to the creek, I was slowly swallowed by a world of green. There were thickets of blackberries, shiny green willow bushes, and tall cottonwood trees. It was cooler than it had been in my backyard, and the air smelled of ripe blackberries, wild mint, and damp earth.

I stopped for a moment to listen to the birds sing and enjoy a mid-morning blackberry snack. The berries were fat and sweet, so I carried a handful along with me as I continued to the banks of the creek.

The berry bushes and willows gave way to the tall, green grass that lined the creek's edge. I stopped for a moment. Without thinking much about it, I broke off a tall milkweed stalk so that I could watch the end bleed the thick white sap that we thought looked just like milk. I was listening for other kids, but it was quiet except for the soft gurgling of the creek and the busy chattering of the birds who lived in the thickets.

This particular part of the creek was always special in the early summer. Because there was an irrigation ditch on the other side, the farmers had to bring in a tractor every spring to build a dam, which diverted water to their ditch. We kids automatically ended up with a swimming pool, because the rock and gravel dam created a pond that stretched a hundred yards or so upstream.

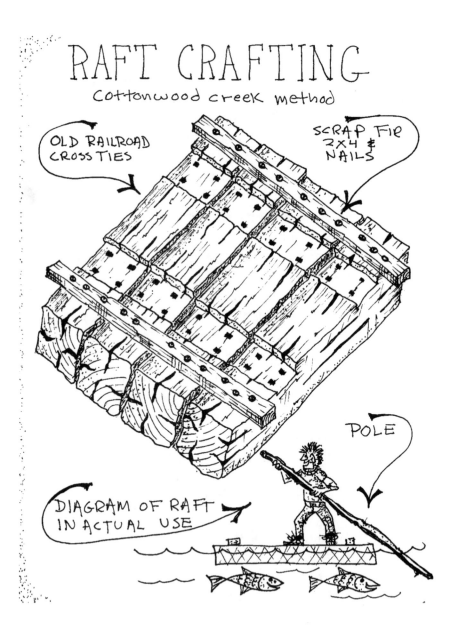

It was good that there were no other kids around, because that meant that I could use our raft for a little boat trip up the creek. The raft was simply five old railroad ties that Willy, Billy, and I had found stacked along the tracks. Experience told us that they were destined to be burned, so we felt free to take a few. We had used my wagon to haul these heavy hunks of wood, one at a time, down to the creek's edge. Once we got five ties all together, we got some hammers and scrap two-by-fours from home and nailed crosspieces on to hold it all together. We usually had to do this every year, because the spring floods always moved our rafts down to the Klamath River. (We hoped some other kids would use it next year.)

I leaned my BB gun against a willow bush. After locating the pole that we had cut to push ourselves around with, I used it to pry the raft off the bank and into the water. Once it floated freely, I jumped onboard with the pole in hand. Because railroad ties are heavily soaked with creosote, this thing tended to sit somewhat low in the water. But, since I knew that Mom wouldn't get mad if I came home with wet tennis shoes, I pushed on out into the creek.

Ever so carefully, I poled the raft around until it pointed upstream. It was slow and sluggish, but I was afloat and that in itself was fun enough. As the channel narrowed, I moved into the shadows of the willow thickets that lined the creek. On the sandy bottom, I could see trout darting here and there; and in the shady holes by the tree roots, there were groups of suckers feeding on the sandy bottom.

Because I was moving along so slowly, the birds waited until the final moment to flee as I invaded their shady hiding places. For a long moment, I stopped and enjoyed the cool shadows, wondering if this was how Tom Sawyer felt when he rafted the Mississippi River. Too bad my creek wasn't a bit bigger so I could just float on down to the Klamath River...and then on to the ocean...and then maybe on to Hawaii or Japan.

Ever so slowly, the current eased me back to where I had started. With a few expert pushes of the pole, I guided the good ship "Railroad Tie" back toward her resting place. As I neared the bank, I stood at the rear of the raft, raising the front end and making it easier to pole it up onto the bank.

On shore I grabbed my BB gun and headed down stream. Because the water wasn't very deep this time of the year, it was easy to wade to the other side. As I crossed the creek, something caught my eye. My heart skipped a few beats. My footsteps had startled a water snake and it was racing across the creek to get away from me. We all knew that these yellow striped beauties were harmless, but all snakes scared the heck out of me.

Quickly I brought my BB gun to my shoulder and squeezed off a quick shot at the fleeing snake. The splash was a foot too high, so I cocked another load of compressed air into the gun and tried another shot. This time the BB's splash was six inches too low and the slithering reptile took shelter in the tall grass that covered the creek's banks. As I cocked the gun again, I realized that my heart was beating like crazy.

I stood very still for a few moments, just to make sure there were no more water snakes lurking about. My plan was to continue on down this opposite bank in the hope of finding some quail to shoot. There was a covey of big, fat, valley quail that lived in this area. They were never hunted, because it was too close to town to shoot. These particular birds were so fat because Ben Phillips (who owned a service station and a couple of old tourist cabins) had a wife who fed them right along with her chickens.

I figured that, if I could avoid the watchful eyes of Ben's wife, I could knock off a few quail for dinner tonight. As I crept through the berry thickets, I could hear some of the hens clucking—but my heart just wasn't in it. I knew that quail season didn't start for three months and that my parents would be upset about my hunting out of season. Even with a toy BB gun, it was still against the law, and I wasn't eager to become a lawbreaker.

Hopping from rock to rock, I crossed back to the other side of the creek. I had my eyes on a clean, smooth mound of sand that was invitingly shaded by a large willow tree. It was the kind of spot that seemed to cry out, "Come and rest in my shade and enjoy my view." The sand was soft and clean, and the tree was perfect to lean against; so there I sat, with my Red Ryder rifle cradled in my lap.

As my eyes scanned the bushes and trees for signs of wildlife, they suddenly focused on something man-made sticking out of a pile of driftwood. It was a couple of short two-by-fours nailed together, with a faded yellow broom stick nailed on top, sticking out about two feet. The broom-stick had an upright nail in the end.

I smiled to myself. This collection of boards was a war relic—a homemade Browning 50 caliber machine gun. It was a leftover from the days when this very patch of blackberry jungle had been transformed into the battlefields of Iwo Jima, Guadacanal, and Guam all rolled into one.

Because this had happened over six years ago (when I was just a little kid) and the big war was still going full blast, it was a hazy memory. But I could still recall how the big kids (Gene Breceda, Wayne Paulsen, Al McCann, Jay Williams, and the Duncan boys) had played in this area. They dug real marine foxholes and built roofed bunkers with wooden machine guns mounted in pillbox like openings. The trenches were also interconnected with a maze of tunnels they had hacked into the blackberry thickets.

The battles would often start after school. We little kids would be walking home with our lunch pails in one hand and our finger paintings in the other hand. The big kids would roll up on their big bicycles and start recruiting us for their marine platoons. It's hard to be a captain of an infantry platoon unless you have some troops, so the recruiting was

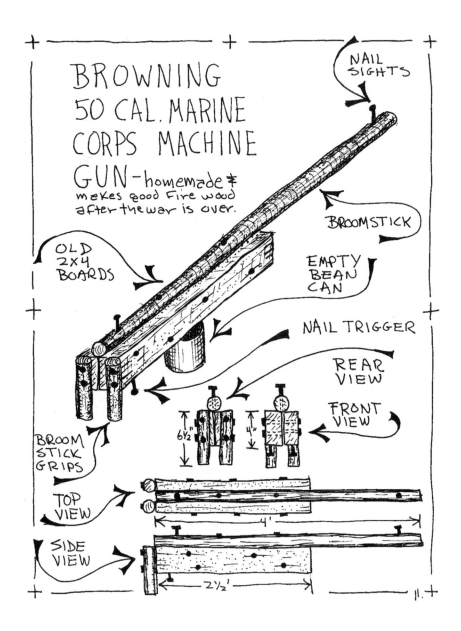

BROWNING
50 CAL. MARINE
CORPS MACHINE
GUN—homemade ⚡
makes good fire wood
after the war is over.

NAIL
SIGHTS

BROOMSTICK

OLD
2X4
BOARDS

EMPTY
BEAN
CAN

NAIL TRIGGER

REAR
VIEW

FRONT
VIEW

BROOM
STICK
GRIPS

6½"   4"

TOP
VIEW

SIDE
VIEW

4'

2½'

11.

58

important. Then, we'd all come down here with our homemade rifles and our cowboy cap guns and the battles would begin.

When someone would shout "Bonzai," this was it. We were under enemy attack. Ktchu-ktchu-ktchu-ktchu. The machine gunners fired their broomsticks at a furious rate. We riflemen fired our wooden M1's as fast as we could pull the triggers. When we thought that "the enemy soldiers" were really close, we'd pick up our grenades, which looked a lot like creek stones, pull the pins with our teeth, and hurl them overhead just like John Wayne.

A couple of times, I took a "hit" and Billy Paulsen would be the corpsman and administer saccharine pills he had "borrowed" from his mom. The healing was immediate and we nearly always won our battles with the hordes of samurai warriors who lurked in these jungles. It was a pleasant way to wage a war; you always got to go home to a warm supper and your own cozy bed.

I jerked my head and slapped my cheek. The darn mosquitoes had found me and that meant I had to move on down the creek—or end up being lunch for these pesky bloodsuckers. Reluctantly, I left my sandy resting place and threaded my way back through the willow thickets to the creek bank.

From time to time, I stopped to examine prints left in the soft mud by raccoons. It was rare that we ever laid eyes on a coon or a skunk, as they were mostly out and about at night.

In places where the creek ran slowly, there were lots of spider-like insects that skittered about on the surface of the creek. We called them "Water Skippers" and it was great sport to shoot them with a BB gun or a slingshot. The splash always told me how close I hit, but it was nearly impossible to hit a skipper. After about ten or fifteen shots, my arm got tired from cocking the BB gun, and I started meandering down the stream again.

As I neared the fishing hole, just upstream from the bridge I saw that someone was fishing. This was a fairly good spot to fish and, because it was close to downtown and close to the bridge, it was also a popular spot. As I came through the willows, I saw that it was Norman O'Donald standing in the creek with his fishing pole in hand.

Norman (who was about twenty-five years old) lived with his mom up the hill. We knew that he had never graduated from high school and still didn't have a job. He lived kind of like us kids, except he didn't have to go to school. We all knew that Norman had some sort of problem with learning things, but people didn't talk about it much. The main thing was that Norman was kind to us; so we went out of our way to be friendly to him by always asking him about whatever he happened to be doing.

As I slipped out of the willows, Norman looked up, smiled a little smile, and said, "Hi, Billy." I walked along the bank so as not to disturb his fishing and asked if he had caught anything. He smiled again (it was a proud little kid kind of a smile), reached into his wicker creel, and pulled out two rainbow trout. I said, "Nice going, Norm," and told him he ought to try to get his mom to cook them up for his supper tonight.

I stood and watched him cast for a while. We talked fishing talk, like, "Whatcha using for bait?" and "Which hole did you catch 'em in?" If it looked like fishing was good, I just might want to go home, get my pole, and try to catch a few myself.

After watching a while longer, I climbed the stairs that ran between the bridge and the water company's pump house. Once I was up on the road, I started crossing the bridge the special way that kids always used to cross this bridge. It was built with two iron spans, which were supported on either side by boxed-in iron arches that were about a foot wide and, at their highest point, about six feet from the bridge surface.

If at all possible, you never just walked across this bridge; you always took a little running start and then walked across the top of the iron arches. It was kind of like walking a tight rope. We sometimes talked about trying it on our bikes, but I never knew of anyone brave—or foolish—enough to try it that way.

I ran down the last bridge arch and, still running, turned right to cross the street so that I could go into the back door of T. Jones' store. The old screen door bammed behind me and I immediately noticed how cool it was inside. I wandered off to the left, past Mr. Smith's office with the fancy iron bars over the counter. The big wood stove that Mr. Smith used to heat the entire building was cold today.

In the winter we always detoured through the back door of T. Jones & Company for a quick warming stop by this big old stove. The nicest thing about the stove was that it had a big flat top that was just about at our chin level. When the stove was extremely hot (in the dead of winter), we would stand there and spit onto the big flat top. The little balls of spittle would hiss and bounce and dance a crazy little dance all over the hot stove top. The kids in big cities, like Yreka, had things like pinball machines, but watching little balls of spit dance around on this stove top was almost as much fun. And besides, it was free.

I stayed to the left side of the store and walked up behind the meat counter where "Mac" McCann was carving away at a big hunk of beef. Next to the meat counter was a glassed-in candy counter.

As I slowly looked over the candy display, Mac glanced over and asked, "What are you up to today?" When I told him that I'd been down by the creek, he warned me to "watch out for snakes down there." Mac was known as the best fisherman in town; however, because he didn't have much love for rattlesnakes, he always carried a pistol. Finally, I decided to spend my nickel on an Eskimo Pie from the freezer counter, paid Mac, and headed out the front door toward home and some lunch.

I crossed the street toward the railroad tracks after checking to see if we had any mail in our box at the post office. When I came to the tracks, I hopped along on the wooden crossties for a while; then I walked along on the shiny top of a rail, balancing myself with outstretched arms. It was slower going, this balancing act, but it was much more interesting than just walking home.

After I passed by Willy's house on my right, I hopped off the track and headed on over toward our house. As the front screen door banged behind me, the smell of bacon told me that Mom was fixing up some bacon, lettuce, and tomato sandwiches for my sisters and me to have for lunch.

As I leaned my BB gun in the corner and slumped into my chair at the kitchen table, Mom looked up from the stove and asked, "What have you been doing?" I looked back at her and responded, "Nothing much."

Chapter Six

A Boy and His Rifle

In the summer time, our front porch was by far the best place to eat lunch. One sunny morning, I made myself a salami sandwich with soft white bread, mayonnaise, and lettuce and poured a big glass of milk. Then I headed for the front door so that I could get myself all set up in the big wooden chair that Dad had just made especially for the front porch.

As I sat in the shade and ate, I could watch the Southern Pacific steam engine shunting railroad cars up and down the tracks that lay across the open field from our house. The brakeman hopped off a moving car, inserted his key into the big brass padlock on the switch, pulled the lever up, and tugged it around to realign the tracks. Then he pushed the lever down, locked the padlock, and signaled the engineer with his arms. The locomotive chug-chugged softly a few times, then rolled easily down toward the sawmill to pick up some carloads of freshly planed Douglas fir.

I heard the solid "klunk," as they connected with the lumber cars, and more chug-chugging, as they came back up by our house to rejoin the main line. Soon the train was complete and they started up the hill toward Oregon.

Train watching wasn't a really big hobby of mine, but it sure made sitting on the porch and eating lunch an interesting activity. There was something about a steam locomotive that always caught my attention. Even though they were a common sight, there was always something fearsome and scary about them.

Once the train had chugged up the hill, things got quiet again. All I could hear was an occasional dog barking and the chirping of some sparrows perched high up in our big locust tree.

As I finished the last bits of my lunch, my mind turned again to my most immediate goal. With school out and the whole summer ahead of me, one major test of young manhood stood between me and my days of summer fun. I had yet to convince my dad that it was okay for me to take his 22 rifle on my hikes without his personal supervision.

At my age, not being able to go out on my own with a rifle was like not having a bike when I was younger. My dad wasn't a really strict parent, but he was very careful of firearms. I knew I had to muster up all the persuasion my 11 1/2 year old brain could think of for this little project.

For several years, Dad had taught bits and pieces of rifle safety to me. On family picnic trips up the Klamath River, he would set up an empty baked bean can and let me and my big sister, Sally, take turns shooting at it. The biggest thrill of all happened one evening on the way home. I got to be the one to get out of our old Chevy and shoot the rattlesnake who was unlucky enough to have been crossing the road as we happened by.

I knew that you never had a loaded gun in the house or in the car. I also knew always to carry it on safety, pointed at the earth or toward the sky. Dad had demonstrated many times the correct way to crawl through a fence with a gun and how always to check that my shots were backed up before I squeezed that trigger. A 22 rifle is a complicated sort of toy, but, for me and my friends, it was as important as a baseball mitt or a bike. I just knew I was ready for this.

Dad was working the 8am to 4pm day shift at the Agricultural Inspection Station on the California-Oregon border, so I had a few hours to kill 'til he came home. Cleaning the rifle seemed like a good way to pass the time; and it would show Dad that I was the kind of guy who would take good care of his Winchester. As I dragged a chair over to the kitchen cupboards—so I could reach the rifle in its special hiding place—I was thinking about what Dad had told me about buying the gun in the first place.

Back in the old days, before the war and even before he was married, Dad had worked as a reporter for a newspaper in Flagstaff Arizona. While he was there, he bought the rifle to hunt tree squirrels. Flagstaff was also the place he first started dating a young school teacher named Mom.

The rifle was a Winchester model 09, 22 caliber pump. It had an open hammer and held up to ten rounds of long rifle ammunition in the tubular magazine. It was light weight, easy to carry, and I loved it.

After retrieving the rifle, I covered the kitchen table with old newspapers from the top of the fridge. Then I went to the back porch to find our gun cleaning stuff. A finger-operated screw on the side of the rifle, near the trigger enabled me to break the rifle into two sections for cleaning. Carefully, I poured some Hoppe's Gun Solvent onto a cotton patch and wiped the burned powder from the reloading mechanism. Then I soaked another patch in the solvent and rammed it through the barrel with the cleaning rod. The final step was to repeat the process using Hoppe's gun oil. It smelled like grown-up stuff, and there was no other smell quite like it.

When I finished with the cleaning, I put the two parts of the rifle back together again. Then I put it to my shoulder, sighted at one of the chickens in the back yard, and worked the pump action several times (enjoying the feel and the sound of the solid metal parts clicking into place).

With a sigh of anticipation, I carefully clicked the hammer back to the safety position and laid the Winchester back into its special place on top of the kitchen cupboards. Then I went to my room and got my library book, Thirty Seconds Over Tokyo, and went back to the chair on the front porch for some reading and waiting.

After supper Mom and Dad always settled into their favorite chairs in the living room for some reading. Finally, I decided that the casual approach might be the best thing to do. I just strolled into the room and said, "Hey, Dad, okay if I take the 22 on a little hike up past Jacobs' Hill?" He lowered the newspaper that he was reading, paused for a moment, and said, "Sure, pal, go ahead." Mom gave a "what's going on here" look over her new *Reader's Digest*. But she hadn't said anything yet, so I quickly went to the kitchen, grabbed the rifle and a box of shells, and headed out the back door. I fully expected one of them to call out for me to "wait a minute," so I walked real fast through the back yard.

Once I had hiked beyond Jacobs' Hill, I slowed a bit. Here I was, alone with the rifle but there wasn't much day left to enjoy the experience. The sun was low over Cottonwood Peak and the hills were quiet except for the soft coo-cooing of a dove or two. I sat on a rock on the edge of a small ravine that eventually led to Mossy Falls.

The ground squirrels must have known that I was coming because not a one dared show his head. Not wanting to go home without shooting at something, I took a few shots at a rock across the ravine just to hear the noise, smell the burnt powder, and see the bullet smack on the rocks.

Feeling very grown up, I slowly headed home in the lengthening shadows. The distant sound of a quail rooster calling his covey together drifted down from the hills behind me. I was feeling very complete. I knew that the rifle was more or less mine now; Dad had trusted me with it on my own. I smiled inside because if felt good to be trusted and I hoped that, someday, I'd have a son to pass my rifle on to.

As I lay in bed that night, listening to the crickets sing their songs, my mind was running wild with thoughts of things I could do—now that I could go out with my rifle. Hiking had always been fun, but hiking and hunting ground squirrels and jack rabbits was true adventure. Because it was early summer and because the hills and mountains and creeks started at our back doors, the possibilities seemed endless. As I finally drifted to sleep, a plan was beginning to form in my mind's eye.

Today was Boy Scout meeting day. That was good because it meant that I'd get to see all of my friends at once, without the pain of having to go to school to do it. Because my dad helped keep the troop going, I always had a ride to the meetings. The ride was important because the troop meeting place was clear across town in the old Grange Hall. In addition to having the built-in ride, I also felt proud that my dad helped the troop.

At the meeting, I cornered Oliver and Frank Fick and laid out my plan for a back-packing trip up to Pine Flats. To make it sound more official, I presented it as sort of a Boy Scout trip; and it really would be because that's the way most of our outings got started. Oliver said that he had to work in Mr. Bloomingcamp's hay field, but Frank liked the idea and said that he'd ask his mom if he could go. Next, I talked to Willy Jones and Billy Paulsen. They immediately liked the idea, so we decided to pack our gear the next morning and leave right after lunch time.

On the way home I casually mentioned to Dad that some of us were going on a Scout trip up to Pine Flats the next day. He thought that sounded like the kind of thing a kid ought to be doing in the summertime. No mention was made of the rifle, but I knew that he knew that I knew it was now okay for me to take it along.

The next day, I awoke early, eager to start packing for the trip. After a bowl of Wheaties—the breakfast of champions— and homegrown strawberries, I headed for the garage to find my camping gear.

The first thing I needed was my pack frame. My dad and Mr. Barnum had arranged with a local man for some help in making these pack frames for the Scouts. We made them out of two vertical one-inch square frame pieces, joined

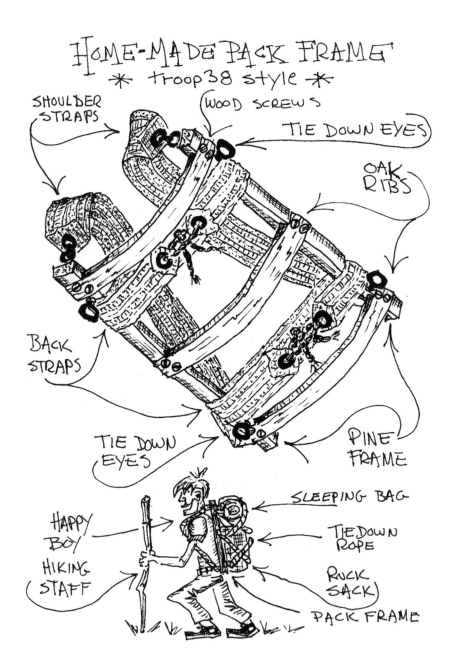

horizontally by three oak ribs. We had arched the ribs to fit our backs by soaking them in hot water, bending them around some nails driven into a plank, and then letting them dry in the sun. The shoulder straps and back straps were furniture webbing purchased from the upholstery shop in Yreka. It was a basic affair, but we made them with our own two hands. And we were especially proud knowing this was the way real men carried their gear back in the gold rush days.

I took the pack rack out to the front porch and then went back to the garage, passing Mom's vegetable garden, to find my canteen and my sleeping bag.

I was really proud of my sleeping bag because it was given to me by my Uncle Bill, who happened to be my favorite uncle. During the war, Uncle Bill had patrolled the ocean beaches for the U.S. Coast Guard. With a rifle and a Doberman named Peachy, he had watched to make sure the Japanese didn't land any troops on the Oregon coast. My genuine goose down mummy bag was once part of his equipment, so it had actually been in the war with someone I knew. Light weight, with a waterproof cover, that bag was one of my most prized possessions.

I dusted the bag off and carried it and my fire-blackened cook kit out to the front porch. One more trip for my green canvas Boy Scout pack sack and my canteen, and I was ready to start thinking about what I was going to eat for the next two days.

I hopped on my bike and coasted down the hill and across the railroad tracks toward the T. Jones & Company store. I skidded to a stop, leaned my bike against the front wall, and went inside to find our neighbor, "Mac" McCann, who was both the butcher and a clerk. Inside the old brick building it was cool, dark, and full of the smells of oiled wood floors, celery, onions, and nuts and bolts.

With Mac's help, I was soon on my way home with four cans of chocolate milk, two cans of Vienna sausages, and a large can of Chef Boyardee spaghetti. Most important, I also had a box of hollow point 22 long rifle shells. Everybody in town had an account at T. Jones, so I just charged everything and would give the receipt to Mom when I got home.

Back home I added a couple of peanut butter and dill pickle sandwiches to my collection of canned foods. I then stuffed it all into my backpack along with a sweatshirt, some extra gym socks, and my new *Terry and the Pirates* comic book. Next, the sleeping bag and the full pack were laid on the pack frame and lashed in place with a piece of cotton clothesline rope I had found out in the garage. All I had to do was fill my canteen with fresh water and I was ready to hit the road.

Hornbrook sits in a valley with Cottonwood Creek running down the middle. Lucky for us kids, there are mountains on both sides of the valley. Normally I hiked on the east side of the valley because the hills started almost at my back door. My side of the valley had Horn's Peak, Jacobs' Hill, and endless oak and juniper trees. Pine Flat was located in the higher pine and fir forests on the east side of the valley.

My next task would be to round up Willy and Billy so that we could hike across town to Frank's house and on to the edge of town and the mountains beyond. It only took me ten minutes of biking and talking until we had an agreement to meet at Mrs. Kurt's candy store right after our moms fed us lunch. From there the three of us would walk together on over to Frank's house.

After lunch, I grabbed my new navy blue baseball cap and headed for the front porch with the rifle in hand. I strapped my war surplus canteen and hunting knife around my skinny waist and stuffed the box of 22 shells into my jeans pocket. Finally, I wrestled my pack rack onto my shoulders, said good-bye to Mom, gave our old dog, Mickey, a scratch behind the ears, and headed down the street toward the railroad crossing.

As I whistled and walked along, trying to balance myself on a railroad track, I was one happy Boy Scout. I had a rifle in my hand, everything I needed on my back, and two days of total freedom and adventure in front of me.

As I began to cross the bridge over Cottonwood Creek, the smells of cool water, blackberry bushes, and moist willow thickets caused me to slow to a stroll. This was always a pleasant place to be. In the middle of the bridge, I stood next to the railing and stared down at the snow-fed waters.

Without thinking too much about it, I slowly moved about a foot to my left so I would be exactly above a round rock standing a few inches above the water. Carefully, like a B-17 bombardier, I released a wad of spit toward the rock. A small air current curved my projectile a few inches away from the target. I moved back to my right a few inches, aimed and dropped another spit-bomb. This time I scored a direct hit, so I left the bridge feeling rather proud of myself.

On up the hill a bit the road led me to Mrs. Kurt's candy store. There, I found Willy and Billy sitting out front, enjoying tall bottles of Pepsi and Planter's peanuts. I dropped my pack on the bench out front and went inside through the screen door to stock up on a few candy bars. As Mrs. Kurt patiently took my assorted nickels and pennies, she inquired about our plans—and warned us to be careful. I put a few Tootsie Rolls into my jeans pockets and stashed the rest of my candy in my backpack for future enjoyment.

Now we were the Three Musketeers, as we donned our packs, grabbed our rifles, and trudged up the road past our little white church and on up around the bend where the Burns girls lived. When we saw a straight stretch past the town cemetery and the rustic sign that noted where the stagecoach station had once stood, we knew that we were approaching Frank's house.

Frank had seen us coming down the road, so he was already sitting on his front porch playing toss ball with his collie dog, Lassie. Once Frank packed up and told his mom he was leaving, we were really on our way. Only a few more houses and we'd leave the town behind us, and being out of town was what this was all about.

The first hill was always the hardest, especially with a backpack biting into my back. But no one complained as we climbed the old dirt road that led to the trail. As the road leveled a bit, we stopped for a rest and a quick look back across the green alfalfa fields and scattered pine trees in the valley below. It was truly a beautiful day, with clear blue skies, a gentle breeze, and the smell of pine growing stronger with every step.

A few more yards and we dropped off to our right into the canyon that held Rancheria Creek. Because the afternoon sun could not reach this area, leafy trees grew abundantly and suddenly it became shady and cool as we hiked the old trail. This was a good place to be and we were all happy to be on the trail.

As we walked along the creek, the young maple trees reminded me of a Hornbrook mystery that always sent little shivers up my spine. Deep in our cemetery, on the left side where the old sandstone markers stood, there was one odd grave. The stone simply stated, "Woman Found Hanging in Tree." Town legend had it that she was found hanging by the neck from one of these very maple trees back in the Gold Rush days.

This was such an odd story that it seemed almost like a fairy tale. But, the fact that I had seen the tombstone many times gave me a scary feeling when I hiked through this area. I believed in God and believed in Jesus and I didn't believe in ghosts, but I still didn't like thinking about trees with bodies hanging in them, so I kept on hiking.

Further up the canyon, we crossed over the creek to inspect an old gold mine. Our moms and dads had all warned us not to fool around in old caves, but there was just something about a hole in the ground that excited our curiosity. This particular cave was not too deep and had some water in it, being so near the creek. Slowly, one by one, we ventured into the darkness. In the cool, misty, and drippy dark, visions of sudden rock slides danced in my head. As the light grew dimmer, my fear grew brighter. The soft flapping of a bat's wings started me thinking about sleeping bears and hidden rattlesnakes. Suddenly our bravery evaporated and we hurriedly retreated into the blinding afternoon sun.

Once we were all outside again, I lifted my rifle and fired three quick shots into the darkness (just to hear the echo and watch the water splash). We stood there for a moment smelling the burnt powder. Then as one, we headed back up the rocky canyon.

As we hiked past a level spot next to the creek, Frank and I started telling Willy and Billy about an outing Frank's brother, Oliver, and I had on this very spot. Last Easter vacation, Oliver and I had been eager to do something exciting, even though the weather was still cool. We borrowed a Boy Scout pup tent, packed our gear, and hiked up to this campsite for an over-nighter. Frank had to stay home and do chores.

The next morning, we opened the tent flat to find our world covered with snow. On the way up to visit us that morning, Frank had managed to shoot a big fat tree squirrel with his 22 rifle. The three of us spent an hour or so trying to get all the skin and fur off the darn thing so that we could fry it in my leftover sausage grease. In the end, we couldn't get all the hair off the sticky meat, so there wasn't much fighting over who got the biggest share. However, it wasn't a meal we would soon forget, either.

Beyond this point the canyon forked and we knew to take the left side, with its smaller creek. The going got tougher, as there were more rocks and many trees crisscrossed the ever steeper canyon.

My stiff wooden pack frame was biting into my back and my rifle seemed to weigh a ton. My clean white T-shirt was now soaked with honest boy sweat and my lungs were beginning to cry out for more oxygen. Willy and Billy were rapidly pulling ahead, motivating me to keep my skinny legs in motion. As we climbed higher and higher, the pine trees seemed bigger and there were increasingly more Christmas tree firs. My body was throbbing with effort, but my brain never lost sight of the fact that this was the only place that I wanted to be right now.

All of a sudden, I noticed that the hill wasn't quite so steep. In fact, things were getting almost level. I raised my eyes from my dusty tennis shoes to find that we had arrived.

What a great place! Here in the midst of this steep rocky canyon, existed a very level area about the size of a football field. There were many Ponderosa Pines and the ground was thickly covered with a soft carpet of pine needles. A small snow-fed stream meandered through the middle, and steep brushy hills provided protective walls on both sides.

It was so shady and quiet that we felt like we were wandering into some kind of mountain castle. This was more than just a destination. What a special place to be. Best of all, for now it belonged to us.

After we picked out a fire spot near the stream, I got on my hands and knees and started raking pine needles into a sleeping bag sized pile. (Not only are pine needles soft, they also insulate your bed from the cold ground). After I got my needle heap about six inches thick, I set about shaping it the way I had seen it done in my Boy Scout Handbook. I left low spots for my butt and my shoulders and put some extra needles where my head would be. I lay on it a few times to test my work, then I unrolled my down sleeping bag over the form-fitted mat.

Next, we cleared a fire circle about six feet wide and scraped right down to the bare ground—just the way Mr.

Lyons and Mr. Barnum taught us at our last Scout Camporee. We arranged rocks to contain our fire and soon had one burning, using needles and cones as kindling. Carefully, we added branches over the flaming pine cones in the shape of a miniature teepee. Until we finally went to bed, the fire would give us heat, cook our meals, give us light and entertainment, and even provide us with comfort and friendship.

We just lay around and goofed off the rest of the afternoon. Because Frank's step-dad sold magazine and comic books, the Fick brothers always had a supply of coverless comics. Luckily, Frank had stuffed some comics into his pack; so we read, traded books, and chewed on our candy bars for an hour or so.

After a while, Billy took his rifle, aimed carefully straight up, and shot a pine cone out of a tall tree. It quickly turned into a marksmanship contest (there were many cones to shoot at). The fact that we could do this and still lie flat on our backs had a certain appeal to it.

The mountain air and the hike eventually took their toll. The luxury of taking a nap was just too appealing. One by one we drifted off to sleep, as a gentle up-canyon breeze played soft mountain music in the branches of the tall pines.

Darn it! A fly buzzed my ear, and I jerked my head and swatted at it with my hand. I was awake. My legs were stiff from the climb, and the lengthening shadows were giving me a chill. I took a branch and stirred the fire pit until I found some coals that were still glowing a bit. I placed several handfuls of pine needles on the coals and carefully blew some life into the fire. Next, I added pine cones and some small branches until it burned briskly enough to draw the chill out of my body.

The fire acted like a magnet, gradually drawing all four of us into its circle of warmth. I headed for my pack and started digging out my cook kit and dinner stuff. Everyone else did the same thing, and we were soon busily preparing our meals. Willy and Billy both plopped hamburgers into

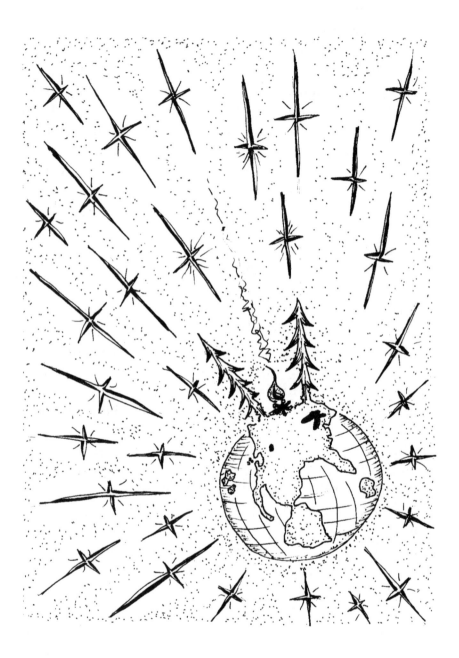

their frying pans, which they then carefully nestled on the red hot coals. Frank pulled out a can of Boston baked beans.

I dug my official scout pocket knife out and opened a can of spaghetti with one of the special blades. After dumping the spaghetti into my little cooking pot, I piled several rocks by the fire. Next, I hung the pot over the fire from the end of a stick, which I rested on my rock pile. Once I weighted the opposite end with another rock, all I had to do was sit there and watch things. Frank did the same thing with his beans, and we waited while our meals heated.

By the time we were through eating, it was totally dark and a lot colder. We burned the fire brighter to push back the chill and the darkness. Silently we just sat there and stared into the mysterious depth of the fire. I'd find a hot looking pocket of heat, poke a branch into it, and hold the burning end above my head just to watch it glow.

We talked about quail hunting and school and airplanes and baseball and even a little bit about girls. With the fire to stare at, no one felt obligated to talk a whole lot. Just gazing into the hot coals was entertainment enough.

I yawned and shivered because my back was cold and my front was hot. Willy carefully laid some larger hunks of wood on the fire in the hope that we'd still have some hot coals in the morning. Frank was the first to announce it was time to "hit the hay" and that sounded good to me.

I gave my body one last warming in front of the fire and headed for my sleeping bag. We just pulled our shoes off and jumped into our bags, clothes and all (it made getting up a lot easier when you still had warm blue jeans on).

Soon we were snuggled into our bags. It got very quiet except for the crackling of our friendly fire. After a while, even the fire quieted down and we just lay there, staring at the sky. The Milky Way was so bright it looked as if you could climb a tree and walk across the sky on it. I picked out the Big Dipper and used the two end stars in the cup to guide my eyes to the North Star.

Eventually, I stared at the stars beyond the stars and then at the vast darkness beyond that. The idea of infinite distance out there was a very wondrous thing. In Sunday School, we had learned from Mr. Funk that the same God who had created this vast sky was so concerned about me that He even knew exactly how many hairs I had on my head. A staggering thought, but also a deeply comforting thought, which soon led me to a deep and contented sleep.

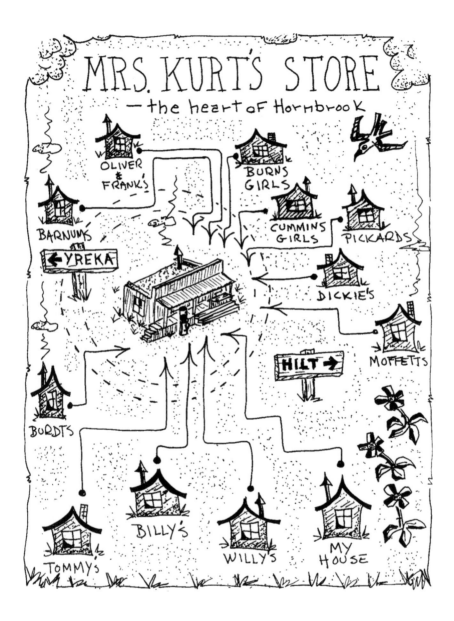

Chapter Seven

Mrs. Kurt's Store: The Heart of Hornbrook

Carefully I poured a little white pool of Wildroot Cream Oil into the palm of my left hand. After rubbing both hands together, I massaged the cream into my dampened hair. I carefully combed a proper wave over my forehead the tried to comb the left side back. Finally, the mirror told me that every hair—even my cowlick—was in its correct place. I was looking mighty good.

I rolled up the sleeves of my clean white J.C. Penney's T-shirt, tucked it into my clean blue jeans, and dusted off the moccasins that I made last month at Lake of the Woods Scout Camp.

One last check in the mirror to make sure that things were perfect, and I headed out the door for an afternoon at Mrs. Kurt's store. As I walked and whistled down the railroad tracks, I quickly noticed how hot it was. Earlier Mom had guessed that it would be over 100 degrees today—a hot day even for August. The more I thought about the heat, the more I thirsted for a tall, cool bottle of Pepsi.

In no time I scuttled across the tracks, past T. Jones & Company, and across the Cottonwood Creek bridge. As I crested the uphill road that ran away from the bridge, the little yellow store came into view.

Mrs. Kurt's store was an old-fashioned sort-of-a-highway-stopping place. Out front it had a big wooden porch, which made a nearly perfect place for kids to hang around. Also out front, it had an old-fashioned gas pump, the kind

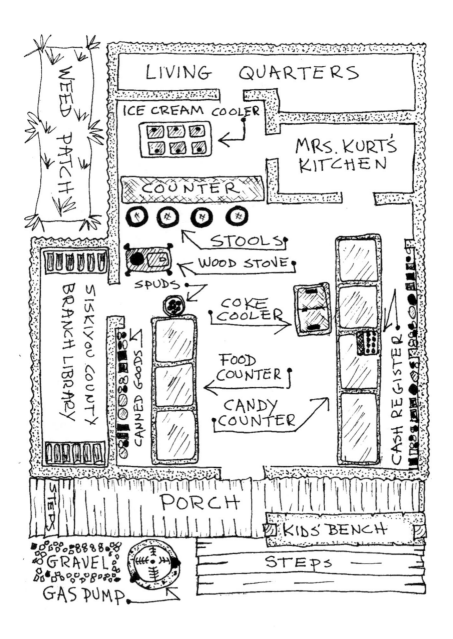

you pumped by hand. On one of the support posts there hung a red signal arm that you could extend to get the Trailways bus to stop for you. The building, covered with corrugated metal sheeting, wore many coats of buttercup yellow paint.

Inside, Mrs. Kurt and her bachelor son, Carl, had an apartment in the back. Off to the left—as you went in—stood a room full of books that served as a branch for the Siskiyou County Library. At the rear of the store part, there was a lunch counter and some stools that mostly served as an ice cream counter; once Mrs. Kurt had served food, but no more. On the left, she stocked a few food items. On the right there was a glassed-in candy counter and a red cooler full of soda pop immersed in chilled water.

In the old days, Mrs. Kurt had worked as a school teacher and had even taught me when I was a real little kid. Now she and Carl just ran this little store on the highway. Every kid in town liked Mrs. Kurt and I guess we felt that she also liked every kid in the whole darn town.

Several things combined to make Mrs. Kurt's store our favorite hang-out. First, the shaded wooden porch with its raised bench made a perfect place for us to sit around. Second, the store was more or less in the middle of town and easy for all of us to get to. Last, but not least, we always felt at home there because of the grandmotherly way that Mrs. Kurt treated us.

As I crossed Highway 99 to the store, I was a bit surprised to see that no one was sitting out front. Once inside, it felt cool and quiet except for the gentle humming of the soda pop cooler. As I lifted the cooler lid to start my search for a tall 12-ounce Pepsi, I heard a voice say, "Hi, Billy." I looked up to see Carl behind the counter and said "Hi" back. After I got my bottle cap off, I paid him seven cents for the Pepsi and two Tootsie Rolls. One nickel and two pennies was all the cash I could scrape up.

BELCH CHART
JUNIOR BOYS FREE STYLE

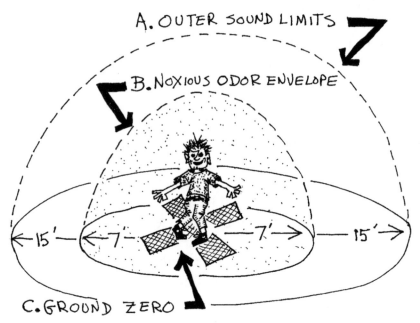

A. OUTER SOUND LIMITS

B. NOXIOUS ODOR ENVELOPE

←15'— ←7'— —7'→ 15'→

C. GROUND ZERO

I. Shown above is a world class effort, scoring 100 points on the Free style scale.

II. For each Foot of shortened sound distance subtract 10 points from total score.

III. Bonus sound points awarded For unusually resonant tones in low Frequency range.

86

As I went through the screen door to the front porch, I saw Dickie Phillipi rolling up on his big new bike. Dickie's dad ran the First and Last Chance bar, which was just down the street (also on the highway). Soon we were both settled on the front porch bench, sipping our sodas and watching the world pass in review on the highway.

After a while we just naturally fell into the "car guessing game." First, I'd say, "I bet a penny that the next car down the highway is a Packard." Then we'd just sit there and see if I was right. Next, Dickie would say, "Okay, I bet a penny that the next car from the north is a Studebaker." Then we'd wait again. Highway watching always had a little edge of intrigue because we could always wonder about the far away places the cars were coming from or going to.

Within a half hour or so, Willy, Billy, Oliver, Frank, and Keith Garret had arrived and were sitting around eating Planter's Peanuts and Cracker Jacks, drinking soda pop, and generally goofing around. Butch Pickard came rolling down the hill on his bike, standing on the pedals. As he pulled in front of us, he stood on his brake, skidded sideways, and sprayed the porch with gravel.

Butch hopped off his bike, climbed the porch steps (with a big grin on his face), jabbed his index finger at Keith, and commanded him to "pull his finger." Obeying, Keith gave the finger a healthy tug, which caused Butch to belch in return.

Not to be outdone, Billy quickly responded with an equally giant belch. Everyone else joined in, laughing and belching and squirting Pepsi at whoever burped the loudest. It didn't get much better than this; but we soon ran out of ammunition and things got quiet again.

Willy got his pocket knife out and began busily carving his initials into the bench. Because so many other kids had done the same thing, it was getting hard to find a place to carve your own mark. Mrs. Kurt didn't mind. She knew that having our initials carved into the bench gave us a feeling of ownership about this place. Occasionally, Carl would put a fresh coat of paint on the bench, but the carving stayed for all to see.

We were all just sitting there, watching Willy carve, when we heard a noise. Oliver seemed to hear it first. It was the sound of girl giggles drifting down the street. As one, we all glanced up the road. Sure enough, here came all three of the Burns girls and the two Cummins girls.

We all pretended that we weren't too terribly interested in girls, but several of us quickly touched up our hair with pocket combs and made sure that our shirts were tucked in nice and neat. We then set about trying to look very unconcerned so that the girls wouldn't think we were overly interested in their arrival.

Once the girls arrived, things changed for the better! There was more talk and more laughter—and much less burping and belching. We were all trying extremely hard to be funny and having a great time doing it. The girls all looked so clean and smooth, and they smelled so fresh.

Just last week at a church roller skating party in Ashland, I had held Arlene Burns's hand during a couples skate. I didn't want to be teased about having a girlfriend, but it was hard to forget how great it had felt to hold a girl's hand.

We giggled and we joked and we teased and we flirted. Time flew on magic wings. There was truly no other place any of us would rather be on this summer afternoon. The front porch of Mrs. Kurt's store just had to be the greatest place in the whole wide world. Too bad we couldn't freeze the clock and spend the rest of our lives right there.

Chapter Eight

The Great Train Ride:
Journey to the Edge of the Unknown

As I wiped the last bit of lunch from my chin, I heard the front gate click open and then klunk shut again. I took a look out of the open front door and caught a glimpse of Oliver and Frank leaning their shared rifle against the front porch.

Quickly, I grabbed my own rifle from the top of the kitchen cabinet, stuffed a box of shells into my jeans pocket, put on my blue baseball cap, and went out to join them.

It was a lazy summer day and we had made some plans to do some ground squirrel hunting. At this point, we weren't too sure exactly who was going or where we were going. We started out by lounging around on the front lawn with some new comic books that Oliver and Frank's step-dad had given them.

After about twenty pages of *Superman* and *Captain Marvel*, we jerked our heads up when we heard a sharp whacking noise from down the street. I knew that noise meant that Willy was out batting rocks with a brakeman's club he had found lying around in a railroad car. I also knew that it meant that he was bored and had nothing better to do.

I decided to get up and walk out onto the graveled street where I could give a shout at Willy. He stopped batting rocks for a moment while I asked him if he wanted to go hunting with us. Heck yes, he wanted to go. He volunteered to ride his bike down to Billy's house and see if he wanted to come along.

I lay back down on the cool green lawn, swapped a comic with Oliver, and went back to reading. About one and a half comics later, Willy and Billy were coming through the gate—rifles in hand.

Because it was so shady on my front lawn and because there were so many new comic books, we all seemed more inclined to lie around and read than to go hunting. Besides, there was always tomorrow or the next day. In the summer time one thing we had was a lot of time.

I had just finished a *Mickey Mouse* when I sensed the faint sound of a train coming into town from the south. Because of the slight upgrade, I could hear the engine working to make it up to the depot for its water stop.

Nothing new about hearing a train come into town, but just lately we all seemed a bit more curious about where they were coming from and where they were going to. Despite dire warnings from our parents, some of us had tried running along and hopping onto a slow-moving box car. We all knew that it was dangerous and forbidden; a fall under those big iron wheels would remove one of your body parts in a bloody second. But the temptation remained.

As we all glanced casually toward the chug-chugging noise, our collective thoughts seemed to be about those great train ride tales that we had heard. These were tales about how the big kids of Hornbrook, Al McCann, Gene Breceda, and Jay Williams, had hopped onto an empty box car and experienced an exciting journey to some exotic place—like Montague or Ashland.

Hearing the stories was one thing, but duplicating these feats was a different matter. There were no handy instruction books on a subject as forbidden as train-ride hitching. And our school principal, Mr. Miller, just never seemed to find it necessary to go to the big kids and assign a five-page essay on the gentle art of train-ride hitching. All we had to go on were the stories we had heard from the other kids.

As one, we noticed that this was a logging train. Now as we saw it, one of the biggest problems to be faced in hopping onto a train was trying to hop off. You just never knew when the darn thing was going to stop. But we all knew that trains loaded with logs were bound for the big sawmill at Hilt.

Our curious eyes took in the fact that several empty box-cars were just sitting there on the siding out in front of Willy's house. It seemed that a guy could hop into one of these cars quite easily without being seen by the engineer. Then the odds would be fairly high that the empties would soon be added to the logging train and moved out of town.

In a magic flash, we all came to the same decision. Every piece of the puzzle had suddenly fallen into place. All that remained was for someone to speak our thoughts. Seeing a nearly perfect opportunity to disobey his step-father, Frank grinned and said softly, "Let's hop the train to Hilt."

We grabbed our rifles and started down the gravel street in a half run. Quickly realizing that our eager pace might call attention from one of our ever-watchful mothers, we slowed to a casual stroll. I even whistled a bit of "Zippity Do-Dah."

We strolled, quite casually, across the field in front of Willy's house to the railroad siding that held three empty boxcars. From time to time, we would throw a glance back toward our houses, just to make sure no parents were watching us. When we reached the train cars, we quickly slid our rifles inside and took turns boosting each other up onto the rough wooden floor.

Once inside, we picked up our rifles and sat leaning against the wall away from the light of the open door—the better not to be seen. Only then did I feel my heart thunk-thunking like crazy. I also realized that this iron box on wheels was going to be like an oven until we started moving. We wouldn't have to wait long, though. The train would either pick us up or leave town with its load of logs as soon as it was through taking on water. In the meantime, we sat quietly while little droplets of sweat dripped off our noses.

From time to time, one of us would move to the door and take a peek in the direction of our houses. Finally, we heard the chug-chugging of the locomotive as the train began to move again. It hissed and rumbled right past our box-car as it began to leave. Then it slowed down. Hot dog! They were stopping to pick up these three empties.

We clearly heard the hissing of the air pipe as the brake-man uncoupled the caboose, and more chug-chugging as they pulled up past the switch. There was a soft chug as they started rolling slowly down the slight downgrade on our siding. We held our breaths until the end car banged against ours. The impact knocked us all flat onto the rough wooden floor. I was so intent on listening to the brakeman's hooking up the coupling and the brake line, that I hardly noticed the splinters I collected from the floor.

It got very quiet for a minute or two, then came another chug-a-chug-chug-chug. Hot diggity dog; we were on our way. We smiled and laughed and patted each other on the back. We really were going on a train ride. There was no stopping us now. We were on our way to Hilt.

As we pulled northward out of town—past the big tin garage where Lawrence Breceda parked the county road grader—we began to feel it was okay to stand in the door. The moving air cooled our sweaty brows and our sense of excitement grew, as the train rolled faster and faster.

Because I had so many times sat on top of Jacobs' Hill or Horn's Peak and watched the train chug out of town, it now seemed strange to be seeing my world in reverse. Maybe this was the way it would feel to see a zoo from inside one of the cages—exciting in a dangerous kind of way.

We klickity-klacked past the "Y" siding where locomotives were shunted up past Mervin McMaster's house, and then back to the main line to turn them around. We could see the high cliffs of Sandy where we loved to go rock rolling. Sandy was also a great place to gather Icknish, a wild herb used by the Indians. As we rolled past the big poison oak thickets where Dad and I hunted valley quail last Thanksgiving, things began to look new and strange. We had traveled beyond our normal hiking limits.

The sudden sight of a small bluff with several ground squirrels squatting on their tails reminded us that we were supposed to be on a hunting trip. We retrieved our rifles from the boxcar floor, then stood side-by-side in the doorway. When one of the little brown rodents came into view, we all blazed away at it with our rifles. Because our private railroad car was rocking back and forth, klicketing-klacking and moving along at forty miles per hour, it didn't make for a very good shooting platform. This was more like a carnival game than hunting, but we loved every minute of it—even if no one was winning any prizes.

When our locomotive started up Baily Hill, we could feel the whole train shudder as it began to slow down. The chugging was louder and there was more smoke blowing back into our faces.

With our rifles empty and no one wanting to bother with reloading, we just sat amongst the empty .22 cartridges and watched the gullies and hills drift by. Occasionally, someone would pick up a brass cartridge and toss it out of the car so that we could watch it bounce along on the gravel below, its shiny sides flashing in the sun.

Toward the top of Bailey Hill, the tracks curved west and crossed over the highway. We all had felt the minor thrill of being in a car driving under a railroad trestle while a train rumbled over us. Now, it felt kind of thrilling to be on a train rolling directly over speeding cars on the highway below. Almost by instinct, we all tried spitting over the bridge railing as we rumbled past, but the train's windy slipstream blew our spit back into our faces.

As the tracks began the slight downgrade into the valley that was home to Hilt, we noticed a doe and her fawn browsing peacefully amongst the pine trees. Several times, we saw large coveys of mountain quail scurrying amongst the scrub oak bushes. With a hunter's eye, I noticed several clearings covered with a particular kind of weed that never failed to attract migrating doves in late summer.

Now that we were older, dove and quail hunting had become a major late summer and early fall activity. We loved the challenge of stalking these elusive little bombshells, and our moms never seemed to tire of baking them for dinner.

As I stood there in the swaying boxcar, trying to figure out how we could come back to this area for some hunting, a story the Fick brothers had told me came to mind. Last October, it seems they took their 16-gauge shotgun and went looking for some valley quail in the big blackberry thicket up in Henley behind Oscar Barnum's house. We all like Mr. Barnum because we knew his kids, Mike and Penney, and because he helped out with the Boy Scouts. But that didn't mean we weren't severely tempted by the fat quail that Mrs. Barnum hand-fed from her back porch every morning.

It seems that Oliver and Frank couldn't flush a single quail on that day, but they did notice that one of the Barnum's geese was straying a bit far from the homestead. Not wanting to return home without some game for the dinner table, they figured that the poor goose was fair game, so to speak. They hauled their kill over to the old Dredger Pond, where they plucked it and cleaned it. After washing the carcass in the pond, they cut the breast into two chunks and reported to their mom, Kathryn, that they had bagged two big rooster quail. The puzzling thing about this whole episode was the fact that Kathryn had served these strange hunks of meat for dinner without any suspicious questions. Parents were getting harder and harder to predict these days.

My daydream was interrupted by the moaning of the locomotive whistle. We were entering the outskirts of Hilt.

Because this was a "company town," totally owned by the Fruit Growers, all the houses were made out of bare wood and looked exactly the same. Even the sidewalks were made out of wood, which meant that no one did much roller skating around here. They had two things in this town that we didn't have though; a little hospital where my big sister had been born, and a community clubhouse that had real pool tables.

I was more than a little bit relieved to hear the screeching of the metal brake shoes as they squeezed against the iron wheels on our car. I guess that part of me just wasn't absolutely positive that we would really stop here, and I didn't want to end up in Oregon. Finally, the train jerked to a complete stop right smack in the middle of Hilt. Willy took a quick look in both directions to make sure there weren't any brakemen nearby. We all hopped out together, then walked quickly across the railroad tracts to a dirt road that led to the company store. Everyone was in the mood for a Pepsi and some Tootsie Rolls.

We sat for awhile on the wooden porch of the store, enjoying our treats. Billy's big brother, Wayne, had driven him up here for some games of pool last week, so he wanted to cross the tracks to the clubhouse and shoot a few games. We talked it over, but the general lack of funds, and the fact that we were all kind of worried about getting back home, swayed us to skip the pool hall. Besides, none of us really knew how to shoot pool anyway.

As we walked up the wooden sidewalk past the church, it was time for some serious thought about getting home. After all, we hadn't done much hitchhiking and most people probably wouldn't stop for kids with rifles. As we walked up the hill past Gino Trinka's service station and the community ballpark, we figured that our best shot was to hike to the Inspection Station on Highway 99. We could then take our chances with my dad, who was working the eight-to-four shift today.

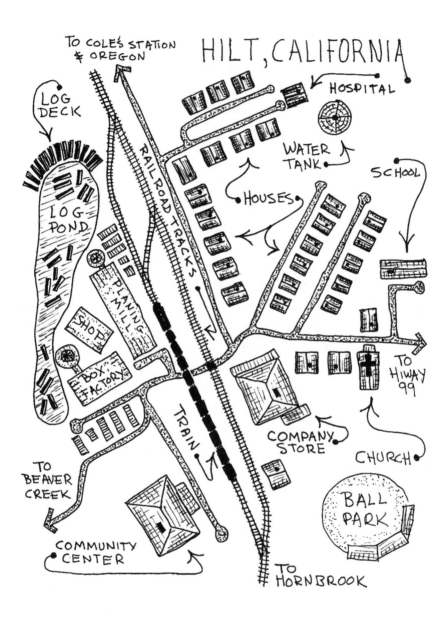

Once we got to the border station, we all just plopped down on one of the big tables at the edge of the drive-through lanes. Dad and Bill Holland's dad, who also helped with the Scouts, were both inspecting a Trailways bus for fruit and bugs. We were all quite familiar with this place because Dad had arranged for the Boy Scouts to come up and make civil defense phone calls a couple of months previously. (When an airplane flew over, we'd spot it with a telescope, run inside, check out the recognition charts, and make the phone call to headquarters. At first it seemed very exciting, but about the eighth or ninth time I called in a "high wing monoplane flying south" the thrill had gone.)

After the big bus roared out in a cloud of diesel smoke, Dad and Dave Holland walked over to us with crooked little grins on their faces. Dave, who also owned Camp Lowe down on the Klamath, said, "Golly, Jete, what do you suppose these boys are doing so far from home?" Dad just smiled and said, "I'm off work in 15 minutes. You guys want a ride?"

After we all piled into our '48 Chevy with the State Farm sticker on the back bumper, things got quiet. We all expected Dad to ask us some uncomfortably direct questions, then give us a lecture about train riding. As we drove under the railroad overpass, we thought for sure the subject just had to come up soon. Finally, I just blurted it out; we had hopped the train. When Dad just grinned, I began to realize for the first time in my life, that he had once been a boy too. Because he hadn't forgotten what it was like to be a boy, he seemed almost to know what I was going to do, even before I did it.

One by one we dropped off all of my friends at their doorsteps. Then, we headed for our house. When I walked into the house, Mom looked up from her mending and asked where I had been all afternoon. I shot a quick glance at Dad and said, "I've just been out hunting." Dad didn't say a word. He just put his lunch box away and sat down in his favorite chair for a cigarette and some time with the *San Francisco Chronicle*. One thing for sure: This was a day I would not soon forget.

Chapter Nine

The Crude Homemade Bomb

I was bored. On Sunday afternoons, the few stores in town were closed, even the post office was closed, and sometimes it seemed like a ghost town. To make matters worse, it was September and that always seemed to be the "no man's land" between summer and fall. It was too late for baseball and the touch football games didn't really get started until the first rains muddied our playing field a bit. Even quail season didn't start for another three weeks, and my Mossberg 20-gauge shotgun was already as clean as I could get it. There was nothing to do but sit around and read an old *Reader's Digest*.

Finally, out of desperation, I grabbed an old baseball, hopped on my bike, and pedaled across the tracks and down toward the silent grocery stores. Just beyond the post office and Mr. Jacobs' store, the street made a right turn toward the Cottonwood Creek bridge. At this point, it went right between the old butcher shop building, which was solid concrete, and T. Jones & Company, which was equally solid red brick.

The smooth, asphalt road and the two opposing building walls made an excellent place to play a little solo baseball. You could throw the ball against one wall, run forward to make a catch, then spin around to repeat the process with the other wall. It wasn't as much fun as playing with someone else, but it would do until something else came along.

I was getting rather hot and sweaty and thinking about going home again when I looked over toward the tracks and

saw Billy walking my way. As he got closer, I could see that he carried a railroad brakeman's club and an old tennis ball. It was great to have some company; Billy started batting his ball against the walls and I scampered to make the catch.

We were both so involved in our game that we hadn't heard the quiet hiss of bicycle tires rolling across the bridge. The sudden screeching of the rear tire on the smooth tar jolted us to a stop. We looked around to see the smiling face of Frank, who was also looking for something to do on this quiet Sunday afternoon. I had seen Frank, and his brother, Oliver, at Sunday school that morning and was glad to see him twice on the same day.

Frank leaned his bike against the concrete wall and announced that he had found a way to get into the old butcher shop building. Billy and I were immediately interested, as we had recently discovered that exploring old barns and buildings could be quite exciting. Because these old buildings were long abandoned, we believed it was okay to snoop around a bit. However, the fact that our parents would probably think of it as trespassing meant that we had to be careful not to get caught. Having to be careful added a certain air of excitement to the whole thing, and we all could use a little excitement today.

A window in the side door had been broken out, so it was a fairly simple matter to reach through and open the door. Once inside, we tip-toed up the stairs to the second floor. There were years of dust and cobwebs—and not really much else— inside. We heard a car go by, with its exhaust echoing off the walls, when all of a sudden I realized that my heart was pounding.

I heard Frank whisper, "Come in here, you guys." I turned left into the side room that he was exploring. In the dim light I could see him standing there in front of an old wooden cabinet, holding a coil of what first looked like black electrical cord. As my eyes adjusted to the shadows, I realized that it was some old dynamite fuse. This stuff was covered with a tar-like substance for waterproofing and the inside was packed with very fine black powder. We had found small amounts of it up at the old Jilsen gold mine, so we knew how to slit the end and light it with a match. Dynamite fuse was fun to have around because you could make really neat pretend bombs and grenades with it.

Because I seemed to be the most interested in our find, I took it home and stashed it away in the workshop that I had built for myself out in the woodshed.

I had just about forgotten the whole incident until one Saturday afternoon a few weeks later. A group of us was hanging around Mrs. Kurt's store, drinking sodas and watching the world go by. Because quail season was just around the corner, we were all talking about shotguns. No one knew more about guns and stuff than Don Burns. As the conversation went on, he mentioned how you could walk right into Cooley & Pollard's Hardware Store in Yreka, tell them your dad needed a pound or two of stump blasting powder, and they'd sell it to you.

It didn't take too long for this possible source of black powder and the fact that I had a coil of dynamite fuse to come together in my mind. So, the very next time that Mom and Dad made a little shopping trip into Yreka, I quickly volunteered to go along "just for the ride."

When we got to town, I announced that I had a "little shopping" to do, then headed straight for Cooley & Pollard's. Once inside the store, I casually wandered around, trying to figure out an innocent way to order two pounds of explosives. I was sure that there had to be some sort of law against this. My problem was quickly solved when a clerk walked up to me and asked if he could help me. Trying my best to deepen my voice to sound older, I quickly responded, "My dad asked me to pick up some stump blasting powder." In no time at all, the cash register cling-clanged and I was walking out the door with a bag full of powdered excitement. I couldn't believe how easy it had been to make the purchase.

The next day was a school day and I could hardly wait to get there so that I could tell Billy, Oliver, and Frank about my purchase. During morning recess, before we started our football game, I told them about the powder. Because no one sold fireworks in California, we became extremely excited about being able to make our own (you had to go to Oregon to buy real fire crackers). We decided to commence our experimentation in my workshop this coming Saturday morning. On the way home that afternoon, I told my neighbor, Benny Raymond, about our project; he was more than eager to help us out.

With something to look forward to, the rest of the school week went by fairly fast. I had just barely finished my Saturday morning breakfast of Shredded Wheat and toast when Benny came knocking at our back door. We sat around the kitchen for a while, trying to decide what sort of materials we might need to make genuine exploding fire crackers. About the only thing we could think of was to seal the ends with melted paraffin, just like Mom sealed her blackberry jelly jars when she canned.

We were just heading out the back door with a block of paraffin and some candles in hand, when Oliver, Frank, and Billy arrived. Together, we walked the flagstone walkway back to my woodshed workshop. We were truly excited, because we were about to start the kind of science project that most boys only dream about. With five guys, a big box of matches, a bag of black powder, and ten feet of dynamite fuse, we couldn't help but have some kind of fun today.

With amazing energy, we spent hours trying to build the perfect homemade fire cracker. We used every kind of building material we could lay our hands on. Each new creation was taken out to the street behind the woodshed and tested. Some fizzled, many just flashed, and several acted more like rockets than firecrackers. Because the stump blasting powder was quite coarse and not very powerful, we really had to work to figure out a way to contain it tightly enough so that it would explode. Even the failures were exciting, though, because we always got a bright flash and a wispy cloud of black smoke for effect.

Finally, through hours of trial and error, we figured out a way to put it all together so that we got an explosion. It was a fairly weak explosion—weaker than a regular fire cracker even. However, the big black sizzling fuse, the orange flash, and the smoke made it look much more impressive than any fire cracker you could smuggle in from Oregon.

By this time we felt that the entire town deserved to be treated to our creations. Besides that, Halloween was just around the corner and we needed to be thinking about testing new trick-or-treat pranks. We decided to return to our homes for dinner, then meet later for some field testing. As we headed for our respective houses, we were dead sure that we had just invented the world's first-ever perfect prank; the homemade firecracker.

Soon, it was getting dark and we were back in my candle-lit workshop. Carefully, we pocketed a good supply of wooden kitchen matches and the three firecrackers that we had managed to build. Then, full of anticipation we set out for a little pre-Halloween trick-or-treating. Only we knew that it was the tricks that were really important tonight.

Our first stop was the street between the old butcher shop and T. Jones. As mentioned in the previous chapter, the solid walls on both sides of the street made a nearly perfect echo chamber, so it was a favorite place for fire crackers. Oliver laid one of our inventions on the tarred street, then Benny lit two matches together. Carefully, he held the flickering flame under the black fuse until it started spitting and sputtering orange sparks. We all moved back a respectful distance and held our breaths. Suddenly, there was a bright flash, a reverberating "POW," and a big cloud of black powder smoke. Big grins lit the faces of everyone all the way around; we just knew that we had finally found the perfect hobby.

Flushed with success and full of high spirits, we headed across the bridge and up the hill. There was no doubt in our minds as to who should be the beneficiary of our second creation. Because it was the only place in town open after dark, the good old First and Last Chance Tavern just seemed to attract us like moths to an open flame. Billy took one of our beauties out of his jacket pocket and carefully split the end of the fuse with his jackknife. He held it while Frank lit it up, then quickly dropped it right smack under the front door. We quickly retreated to the shadows. Then, Flash! Pow! Another one worked like a charm.

In just a few seconds, Angelo (the old Greek bartender) jerked the door open, shook his fist at our cloud of smoke, and shouted, "You darn kids! Get the hell out of here!" Feeling protected by the darkness, we all laughed. Besides, we couldn't imagine that Angelo would call Constable Elmore for something as innocent as a firecracker trick.

By this time, we were overflowing with confidence and our collective sense of adventure was soaring to new heights. Time to try one out on a front porch. Around Halloween time, we always thought about front porch pranks. You could knock on someone's door and then run and hide, or you could rub some soap on their windows. We had always heard that you could put fresh dog poop into a paper bag, light it on fire in front of someone's door, knock, and then run and hide. When they opened the door, they were supposed to try to stomp out the fire, getting dog poop all over their foot. We never tried that one because the fire part sounded a bit dangerous. One that we did try off and on—if we were lucky enough to have a firecracker—was to light one off, chuck it up on a front porch, and then run like crazy.

As we trotted up the street to get clear away from the First and Last Chance, we started debating which porch to bless with our last little invention. We considered both the

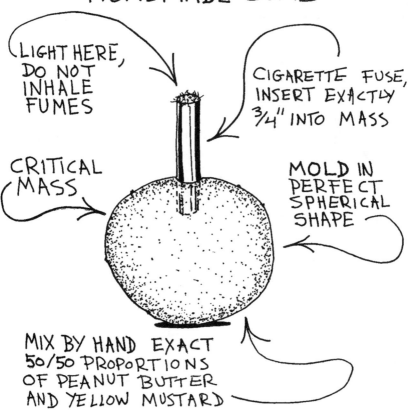

Cummins and the Burns girls' houses as we passed by, but both of those places only had concrete steps and we wanted a real front porch. One of our friends, Agnes VanDeWeigh, lived right across the street from the Burns's and they had a proper porch that was easy throwing distance from the front gate. The VanDeWeighs were friendly folks whom we tended to pick on when it came to Halloween pranks, mostly because we could always count on them to give us a good reaction. A good trick couldn't be a whole lot of fun unless you could get an adult to act angry and shout a few things at you. Judging from Angelo's reaction we should be able to get a real good shout out of Mr. VanDeWeigh.

Carefully, we took out our last home-crafted firework, prepared the fuse with a knife, and lit it with a match. Once the fuse started its sputtering, we chucked it up toward the porch, where it landed with a resounding "thunk." Suddenly our bravery gave out and we all started running like jackrabbits down the street toward the church. The report of the firecracker drowned out the noise of our pounding feet. We knew that Mr. VanDeWeigh would soon be standing at his front door, peering through the cloud of black powder smoke wondering what the heck was going on. Finally, out of breath, we stopped and laughed a good laugh, while we congratulated ourselves for being the best pranksters in the whole wide world.

The next morning, I went to school full of eagerness to meet with my friends and rehash the previous night's excitement. When I saw Oliver and Frank coming through the school yard gate, lunch pails in hand, I ran to meet them. Much to my surprise, there were no smiles, only concern on their faces. Oliver handed me an article from the *Siskiyou Daily News*. Now my smile faded as I read the title, which shouted, "Sheriff Deputies Investigate Crude Homemade Bomb."

Good Lord, something was going terribly wrong here. True, all the tape, paper wrapping, and smoke that our

firecrackers left behind made it seem like a lot more than a Fourth of July "ladyfinger." However, we had to work like heck just to get these things to make a little explosion, let alone act like a "bomb." We couldn't blame Mrs. VanDeWeigh for being upset, but this darn deputy just didn't understand that blowing up a little black powder was standard Hornbrook fun back in the Gold Rush days.

Now I was scared. The term "crude homemade bomb" sounded downright criminal and the fact that a deputy was involved really had me worried. Dad knew we had been experimenting with black powder, so when I finally got home from school I found that he had made some calls and set it all up: Tonight's Boy Scout meeting would be like a trial. We would all meet in the Grange Hall where the "bombed" could openly accuse the "bombers." I just wished I could fake a headache and crawl into bed until this whole thing blew over.

As we parked our nearly new '48 Chevy in front of the Grange Hall, the sight of a sheriff's patrol car set my heart to beating a little faster. Inside the hall, the atmosphere was strained. I noticed that the VanDeWeighs were sitting off to one side with the deputy. I was surprised to see that Pastor Soward was there, dressed in a suit and tie. Next to him sat our scout leaders: Oscar Barnum, Elmer and Al Lyons, and Dave Holland. There was no pre-meeting horseplay tonight. All the scouts were quietly sitting in their folding metal chairs, waiting for the big show.

After Bill Holland and Ray Moffett carried the flags forward and led the Pledge of Allegiance, we stood again and recited the Scout Law and Oath. The deputy seemed about ten feet tall when he stood up, with his shiny badge and that big black gun on his hip. He told us about how this explosive device had invaded the VanDeWeigh's privacy and reckoned it looked to be a downright dangerous sort of thing. I realized in my heart that I really was guilty of scaring the heck out of some decent folks who were never anything but kind to me.

Next, Pastor Soward, who seemed about five feet tall, stood up and testified that he knew these boys and their families. He went on to state that we were basically good boys who didn't mean any harm. Oscar Barnum, who was still wearing his Forest Service shirt with the badge on it, stood. He explained that we may have been guilty of poor judgment, but we surely were not criminals. He was sure that we felt very sorry for what we had done. Deep down inside, I began to realize that being a Boy Scout meant you had four or five fathers, instead of just one. Its was a warm feeling at a time like this.

By the time the meeting was over, everyone had a chance to speak their piece. Somehow, this process of getting together and talking face-to-face had satisfied everybody. As we drove home afterwards, Dad didn't give me any lectures. I guess he knew what it was like to be a boy. He also knew that I had probably had enough for one day.

As I snuggled into the cozy security of my bed, the events of the day were still spinning wild circles in my head. One thing I did know absolutely for sure; I had to find a new hobby as soon as possible.

Chapter Ten

They Never Told Us Kids Were Supposed to Die

The snow had melted and the mud puddles were mostly gone. Mom had even spotted a red-breasted robin. It must almost be spring.

This first hint of good weather had us all out on our bikes. My little sister, Ann, had gotten a new bike for Christmas, so she was really excited that we finally had a good-weather weekend. It wasn't actually a brand new bike from the store. Dad always got older ones and fixed them all up with fresh paint so they looked as good as new.

Ann was the first one out the gate this Saturday morning. We rode our bikes side-by-side down to the post office to see if P.O. Box 176 had any mail in it. I could tell that she was really proud of her baby blue Christmas present, as she peddled along with her pigtails and corduroy skirt waving in the breeze. Ann went home with the mail and I went looking for some of my friends, so we could go biking. After three months of winter, my bicycle and I just had to be on the roads today.

Around midday, I headed toward home, hoping that Mom might have something special for lunch. Sometimes, when we were playing real hard on a Saturday, she would make a pot of potato soup, you know, something to keep our strength up, so we could go back out there and play some more. When I got home, I was a bit surprised to find just my big sister, Sally, there. She told me that Ann had hit a little stone at the edge of the road and had fallen off her bike. Mom and

Dad had taken her to Yreka to see Dr. Schlappi, just in case she needed a stitch or two in the little cut she had gotten on her forehead.

Sally mixed up some tuna for sandwiches. We had just started eating when Mom, Dad and Ann drove up in front of the house. Ann was still rather groggy from the lump on her forehead, so they laid her down on our dining room couch for a little nap. It always seemed as though a good nap could heal almost anything.

Energized by my lunch, I hopped back onto my bike. Sally headed for Jacobs' Hill to see if any wildflowers were blooming yet. Late in the afternoon, my stomach and tired legs motivated me, once again, to head for home. As my tires bumped across the railroad tracks, I hoped that Ann would be finished with her nap. I wanted to tell her that I was sorry she had fallen off her bike.

I could smell dinner cooking when I banged open the front door—that always made me feel good. In the kitchen, I found Mom standing by the stove, looking worried, as she tended the hamburger patties she was frying. When I went back into the dining room to talk with Ann, I was really surprised to find her still asleep. Even more surprising was the fact that she was asleep with one of her eyes open just a little bit. For a fleeting moment, I worried for Ann but Mom and Dad always knew what to do when one of us got hurt. (They had nursed me through three concussions so far.) Parents always seemed to know how to take care of everything.

At the dinner table, Mom and Dad decided that they'd better take Ann back to Yreka to see Dr. Schlappi again. I could see that they were both getting worried that Ann's nap seemed to be going on and on. After they left, Sally and I cleaned up the dirty dishes. For once, we didn't even argue about who washed and who dried.

With the kitchen all cleaned up, we were free to relax and enjoy our evening. I turned on our old Philco radio and spent some time trying to tune in a good station, which was difficult because of the mountains all around us. After a while, Sally got out our Chinese checkers set and we played a few games while we listened to the George Burns and Gracie Allen Show. Finally, tired out from my day of biking, I crawled into my waiting bed. Sally got to stay up a bit longer, because she was older and wanted to wait until Mom and Dad came home with Ann. It was comforting to have parents who always knew how to handle our cuts and bruises and colds and fevers.

Once, during the night, I woke up just enough to realize that the noise I heard was Mom and Dad in the kitchen. Comforted to know that they were home again, I drifted back into a deep sleep.

A ray of consciousness was trying to pry its way into my brain. I fought it back for a moment by burying my face deep into my feather pillow. I could hear the handle on the bedroom door turning and knew it was Mom, coming to wake us for a hearty breakfast.

When I rolled over, I was really surprised to see that both Mom and Dad were standing there beside our bunk bed. Because they looked strangely somber, I spent a few fleeting moments trying to remember if I had done something really bad yesterday. By this time Sally, in the upper bunk, was also waking up. Before either of us really had a chance to figure out why both of them were waking us for breakfast, Mom sat on the edge of the bed. She took a deep breath and slowly murmured, "Ann has gone to be with Jesus."

Why was she talking as if we were in Sunday School, and why were the tears fighting their way into the corners of her eyes? I had never seen either of my parents with tears in their eyes before. Overwhelmed by confusion, my brain started rushing in crazy circles, trying to understand what was going on here. It must be an April Fool's joke, and Ann was hiding out in the woodshed while Mom and Dad told us she was gone. Any second now, she'd run through the door with her big smile and yell, "We fooled you! We fooled you!" But this was a cruel joke. We didn't do such cruel jokes in our family. Why were they playing such a cruel joke? Why?

Seeing the utter disbelief and the total confusion all over our still sleepy faces, Dad said it again. "Ann went home to be with Jesus last night." Oh no, oh no, oh no, oh no, my brain was screaming, "Oh no," as it frantically tried not to believe what they were saying. If I let myself believe what they were saying, I instinctively knew that my entire being would be totally overcome by darkness—the same horrible darkness that I was now beginning to see in their weary eyes.

Finally the wall crumbled. I had to let the truth of their words invade my thoughts. I was suddenly enveloped by the darkest, blackest, coldest feeling I had ever felt in my entire life. At first, the darkness in my mind just stunned me, then I cried out as if some cruel bully had punched me in the stomach. I sobbed and cried great huge tears of utter darkness.

Time stood still while we sat there overcome by the dark realization that Ann was gone forever. All the while, my mind was searching for every bit of wisdom that I had. I was trying to find some bit of knowledge that would help me to cope with this terrible dark pain. My teacher, Mr. Leslie, had never given us a class on what to do when your little sister dies. I had never watched a friend try to cope with the death of a family member.

Eventually, a strange thing happened. We slowly dried our tears and started moving about. It was as if I were a robot operating in a slightly different time zone—an unusual sort of strength that enabled me to put on my clothes and wash my face. The darkness was still there, but I had enough of this detached sense of strength to force it back, just far enough so that I could do a few simple things for myself.

There was a tap-tap at the door. It turned out to be Carmen Davis from up the street. Carmen's husband, Bud, owned the planing mill down by Tommy's house. Because Mom and Dad hadn't slept all night, Carmen was going to keep Sally and me occupied for a while so that they could sleep a bit. We climbed into her Buick convertible and drove into Yreka for some breakfast in an old railroad car called "The Diner."

The strange detached feeling continued as the morning crawled by in slow motion. Because of this dark cloud hanging over my heart and the strange new strength I had found to cope, I felt as if I were living in a different world. It was a very select world where the only other people who could understand were people who had also lost a brother or sister.

When we got back home again, I noticed that someone had left a cake and a meat loaf. The rest of the day, various friends and neighbors were softly knocking on our door, murmuring a few words of concern, and leaving casseroles and desserts. It seemed that our grief now belonged to the whole town, and the town was trying to make things easier by making sure we at least were well fed.

Mom and Dad had been making phone calls to grand-parents, aunts, and uncles. Mom told us that Uncle Jim, Uncle Bill and Uncle Paul were even now driving out from Kansas to be with us. Also, Aunt Thelma and Uncle Reid were on their way from Bakersfield. All of a sudden, I had something to look forward to. My Kansas uncles, the Fowlers, liked to tease and have fun and that might help drive some of the darkness away.

That night, sleep came as a great relief. In my dreams I stood at the sink by the kitchen window. When I looked out toward the woodshed, I could see Ann running toward the house with a big smile on her face. "Surprise," she would say, "it was just an April Fool's joke. I'm not gone. I've just been hiding in the woodshed." It was a wonderful dream. Every inch of my body wanted it to be reality and not just a dream.

But daylight eventually came and I had to try once again to find a way to live with the awful truth. The day started with the anticipation that my aunt and uncles would be here that night. Shortly after breakfast, there was more tap-tapping at the door, and several neighbor ladies arrived with brooms and mops. Soon, the whole "Ladies Aid Society" from church was on the job, busily cleaning our house from top to bottom. Again, our town was sharing our grief by lending a helping hand.

Mom seemed quite pleased to have the ladies cleaning her house, but I was beginning to panic because every room had people in it. I began to fear that someone was going to ask me to talk about Ann. I knew that, if that happened, I wouldn't be able to hold back the horrible darkness that seemed so eager to control my thoughts. Suddenly, I just knew I had to be alone. I grabbed my rifle and headed for Jacobs' Hill with my dog, Mickey.

As I climbed the hill, I could feel cool kite breezes from the north. Soon, the wildflowers would sprout and the little kids would be taking bouquets home to their moms. On top of the hill I sat on a rock, cradling the rifle in my lap. With Mickey lying there at my feet, I gazed back over the town for a moment and then it came. I just couldn't fight the darkness any longer. It came crashing into my body and spirit in giant waves. I sobbed and cried and moaned until there were absolutely no tears left.

I sat in silence for a long time. Then, I saw Dad walking up the street. Through the tears, I watched him climb the hill. When he got to where I sat, he just said, "Hi, pal." No words were needed as we both knew why we were there. We stood for a while, looking back over the town. Then, he put his hand on my shoulder and together we walked back down the hill, with Mickey sniffing along behind us.

Late that afternoon our Fowler relatives started to arrive. I was excited to have them around. With all the food and family in the house, it was kind of like a party at first. My uncles would tease us and we would laugh and giggle in response. We knew that we were laughing to try to hide the grief, but it felt extremely good to have a little something to smile about. Because we had a small house and the nearest motel was in Yreka, the Brecedas and the Smiths offered their extra bedrooms for our guests.

In the midst of all the uncle teasing, I overheard Aunt Thelma asking Mom when were going to "view the remains." I had no idea what that meant and no one really bothered to explain it to me. After a while, I figured out that it was a chance for me to see Ann again.

After dinner, we all got dressed up, loaded into our cars, and drove into Yreka to Girdner's Funeral Home. Funeral homes had always been like cemeteries—scary places that you didn't want to walk by at night. I didn't want these places to become an actual part of my life, but it looked as if that was the way it was going to be. I had absolutely no idea what to expect when I walked into that building, so I was surprised to find it quiet and reverent like a church. Mr. Girdner seemed to be a polite and concerned person who wanted to do whatever he could to make us comfortable.

Once we were all together in the waiting area, Mr. Girdner opened the door to a smaller side room. Inside, I could see some flowers and a polished wooden casket, with one-half of the lid standing open. Aunt Thelma put her arm around my shoulders and walked me into the room. There in that shiny wooden box, filled with silken padding, lay Ann. She was all dressed up in her best Sunday School dress and her hands were ever so neatly crossed in her lap.

I was pleased to see her once more but, as I stared at her face, I began to realize that this wasn't Ann. It truly was just

THE HORNBROOK CHURCH

the "remains." It was Ann's spirit that shaped and molded her face to make her look like my little sister. Now that her spirit was gone, it was like looking at a wax doll. It looked like her, but deep in my heart I realized that this was no longer Ann.

The next morning, Aunt Thelma put on Mom's apron and cooked breakfast for all of us. Because today was the day of the funeral, we were getting out our best church clothes. Mom had the ironing board set up so that we could make everything wrinkle-free, and Dad had his shoe shine box out. In a way, being busy seemed to help us avoid thinking about what we were really going to do today. I did a great deal of shoe shining that morning.

When we drove up to the church, I was astounded by the number of cars parked up and down the street. Again, I had that feeling that the town was sharing our grief. Inside we were guided to some chairs that had been reserved just for us. Once I sat down, I could see that the casket was up front in a sea of flowers. The entire church smelled like a flower shop at spring time.

Once Pastor Soward started to preach, I let the darkness overtake me again. This was the place for crying, so I cried until I could cry no more. At the end of his sermon, Pastor Soward opened his Bible and read the words of Jesus: "Suffer the little children to come unto me." Then as the piano played softly, the entire town filed quietly past the open casket for a final look. When our turn came, at last, I really didn't want to stop looking at her. I knew it wasn't really Ann—I knew it was just an empty shell—but being able to see her body seemed somehow better than having absolutely nothing but memories. Down deep I knew that I was grabbing at straws, but it took Aunt Thelma's arm on my shoulders to move me out to the waiting cars.

Slowly, we all drove to the cemetery behind the big black hearse. Folding chairs were set up on the grass next to the freshly dug grave. As we sat and watched, my uncles slowly carried the closed casket from the hearse and softly set it next to the grave. As Pastor Soward preached, "The Lord giveth and the Lord taketh away. Blessed be the name of the Lord," I hardly listened to him.

My eyes were drawn across the valley to the hills where we played so much. Pleasant memories of Jacobs' Hill and Horn's Peak filled my thoughts. Any day now these hills would be alive with new wildflowers. I sure hoped that God had a special "wildflower hill" in Heaven, just for little kids like Ann.

THE END

(MAYBE)

Order Form

QTY.	Title	US Price	CN Price	Total
	Boyhood Along The Brook Called Horn	**$12.95**	**$16.95**	
	Shipping and Handling Add $4.50 for orders in the US/Add $7.50 for Global Priority			
	Sales tax (WA state residents only, add 8.9%)			
	Total enclosed			

Telephone Orders:
Call 1-800-461-1931
Have your VISA or
MasterCard ready.

INTL. Telephone Orders:
Toll free 1-877-250-5500
Have your credit card ready.

Fax Orders:
425-398-1380
Fill out this order form and fax.

Postal Orders:
Hara Publishing
P.O. Box 19732
Seattle, WA 98109

E-mail Orders:
harapub@foxinternet.net

Method of Payment:

☐   Check or Money Order

☐   VISA

☐   MasterCard

Expiration Date: _____

Card #: _____

Signature: _____

Name _____

Address _____

City _____ **State** _____ **Zip** _____

Phone (_____ **)** _____ **Fax (** _____ **)** _____

Quantity discounts are available.
Call 425-398-3679 for more information.
Thank you for your order!